Cortina

IT'S SNOWING!

IN ART FASHION DESIGN

Vittorio Linfante / Simona Segre-Reinach / Massimo Zanella

Marsilio Arte

COVER
Silvia Gherra, *Holidays On Ice*
2025
Ink on paper

ENDPAPERS
Ottavio and Rosita Missoni
Preliminary sketch for knitted fabric
Women's Fall/Winter 1992 Collection
Archivio Missoni

POSTER
Silvia Gherra, *Homage to Gaston Gorde and to my dad*
2025
Paper cut and mixed media

ART DIRECTION
Vittorio Linfante

LAYOUT
7276, Milano

TRANSLATION
Helen Glanville

COPY EDITING
Lemuel Caution

First edition
September 2025
ISBN 979-12-5463-299-4
www.marsilioarte.it

Available through ARTBOOK | D.A.P. 75 Broad Street, Suite 630 New York, NY 10004 www.artbook.com

ACKNOWLEDGEMENTS

Acknowledgements should not be a list of names. Behind each person, there is advice, help, suggestions, and even, why not, heated discussions. For this reason, we would like to thank the Publisher and the entire Marsilio Arte team, who firmly believed in and supported the project.

We would like to express our sincere thanks to all the designers, fashion brands, public and private institutions, archives, collectors, auction houses, and friends who, in various ways, have helped us in the creation of this volume: Giampaolo Allocco, Elena Maria Bajetta, Ludovica Barabino, Laura Bassi, Damiano Basso, Giacomo Bertocco, Nicoletta Bettolini, Gaia Bianchi di Lavagna, Tiziana Bonanni, Benedetta Bonfigli, Alberto Brambilla, Emiliano Camera Grignani, Giovanna Carucci, Stefania Casacci, Carolina Castiglioni, Emma Cavazzini, Carmen Chiminazzo, Eleonora Corongiu, Andrea Corso, Stefania Cretella, Sara Crosta, Carola D'Ambrosio, Cristina Da Roit, Nicola Dal Zilio, Cristina Del Buono, Roberta Dezza, Sylwia Dziewiecka, Filippo Federici, Mariana Franzetti, Leonardo Freyrie, Chiara Fucci, Andrea Fuscaldo, Renata Fusi, Elena Gaiardelli, Eleonora Geppi, Rina Gerbelle, Arianna Ghilardotti, Marina Gigli, Luca Gregotti, Maria Gregotti, Daniela Grignani, Riccardo Guasco, Silvia Jacovitti, Jasmina Kaluderovic, Sophie Kern, Yasuhiro Kobayashi, Stefanie Krisch, Giuliana Ledda, Alberto Leoni, Giovanna Linfante, Mariapaola Linfante, Nicoletta Linfante, Pasquale Linfante, Emma Loison, Enrico Longo, Sabrina Longo, Maddalena Terragni, Simone Mancini, Laura Marino, Serena Meneghel, Giovanni Milazzo, Luca Missoni, Leonora Mistretta, Silvana Mollica, Giacomo Montagner, Elisabetta Montagni, Massimo Moretti, Enrica Morini, Celeste Morozzi, Antonella Narcisi, Marta Paleari, Raffaello Pernici, Silvia Piombo, Stefania Pistolato, Federica Pittaluga, Elisabetta Rastelli, Stefania Ricci, Roberta Robbie Ricciuti, Francesca Rossi, Paolo Rossi, Susanna Rosti Rossini, Roberta Ruozzo, Titina Russo, Barbara Sambri, Francesca Sangalli, Daniela Sardone, Francesca Sfoggia, Giorgio Sonzogni, Rossella Taffa, Khadim Tall, Luca Tavian, Valerio Terraroli, Tania Tommasini, Andrea Torella, Sabina Tutone, Rémi Vallin, Carla Valzelli, Alex Veronese, Marco Zallot, Enrico Zanella, Marco Zanoni, Paolo Zanotto, Camilla Zardin.

Thanks to Attilio and Benedetta Mazzini, Carla Marangoni, and the entire team at Archivi Mazzini for their expertise, kindness, and cooperation over the years.

We want to express our sincere gratitude to Francesca Sfoggia for undertaking this project and providing us with precise and accurate information.

CONTENTS

IN CASE OF SNOW

Vittorio Linfante

Cold, white, silent: snow has always presented two faces to hunanity. One face a barrier and the other opportunity; it is both a hostile and a fascinating element. In the past, winter meant isolation, difficulty in traveling, the slowing down of trade, and a real challenge for survival. But as has often been the case in the history of humankind, where there is an obstacle, invention will follow.

This is precisely where creativity comes into play. Snow ceases to be just a nuisance and becomes a terrain to be explored, first for fun, then for sport. Ice, once only a slippery and dangerous surface, is transformed into a track. Winter, from being a seasonal intermission, becomes a time for self-expression. It is a metamorphosis that speaks volumes for our relationship with nature: not simply adaptation, but also discovery, experimentation, and enjoyment. To walk in deep snow? Much too tiring. Better to slide over it. Thus are born the earliest solutions for moving around more easily: snowshoes for walking and rudimentary skis for sliding. Falling on ice? Dangerous, of course. But what if it all turns into an elegant dance? Enter ice skating. The same is true of sledges and toboggans: initially means of transport, then a means to experience the thrill of speed. Snow and ice, once natural obstacles, become an invitation to play, explore, and imagine new movements.

Winter becomes an open-air laboratory. Where once it was only a question of survival, a new dimension comes into being: that of performance, pleasure, and challenge. It is the beginning of a long journey in which creativity and the cold merge together, transforming the landscape into an experience to be lived.

HISTORY AND RISE OF WINTER SPORTS

Long before skiing became a sport, an accessory to catwalks, or took the spotlight in publicity campaigns, skis were an implement used in the vast snow-covered expanses of Scandinavia. Skiing was a means of transport, a natural extension of the body to cross snow and ice. Hunting, getting around, surviving. One of the earliest examples of a ski was discovered in Sweden, and is believed to be 5,200 years old, while one of the first images of a skier is about 4,000 years old and was discovered in Rødøy, Norway. It is an image of a stylized human figure with feet resting on two strips about two and a half times its height.

While the first signs of skiing as a sporting activity date back to 1880, with races such as the Nordenskiöldsloppet in 1884 in northern Sweden, between the villages of Jokkmokk and Kvikkjokk, won by the Sami skier Paava Lars Nilsson Tuorda (who came first out of eighteen participants, covering the 220 kilometers of the race in 21 hours and 22 minutes), other competitions, such as the Vasaloppet and the Norwegian Birkebeinerrennet, followed in the 1920s and 1930s. The organization of skiing as a sport picked up speed in the early decades of the twentieth century with the formation of national ski associations in Sweden (1908) and Norway (1908), and that of the International Ski Federation (founded in 1924 in Chamonix, with the first Winter Olympics), which represented the beginnings of a unifying body for the sport. It would only be at the turn of the nineteenth and twentieth centuries that, in parallel with urbanization and the altered relationship with nature, skis—as well as skates, snowshoes and sledges—began to evolve from being a means of transport to also playing a recreational role. This led to the emergence of Winter Carnivals in Canada and North America, and more generally in cold regions with their long winters that harbored a desire for getting together in the coldest months also. These were large popular festivals where the snow became the setting for competitions, parades, ice sculptures, and improvised sports. One of the earliest and most famous was the Quebec Winter Carnival, already in place in 1894, which became one of the largest winter festivals in the world. Legendary editions of this festival would be held in Montreal as early as in the 1920s, and in the United States, the St. Paul Winter Carnival, in Minnesota, which came into being in 1886, quickly became a regular event, with monumental ice castles and competitions on ice and snow.

It is here, between Canada, the United States, and Europe, that winter sports assumed the form of a collective and social experience, rather than a tool associated with strenuous exertion. Skiing and winter sports in general became more widespread, and individual disciplines began to take shape: alpine skiing, cross-country skiing, ski jumping, figure skating and speed skating, skeleton, sledding, tobogganing, and ice hockey. Each sport was born from a simple idea: to slide, to glide, and move fluidly on terrain that normally impedes movement. Many of these sports, while retaining their Nordic or Alpine origins, develop into vehicles for local and regional identity. Hockey becomes the soul of Canada, ski jumping a symbol of the Norwegian valleys, and slalom viscerally linked to the Alpine arc.

What was once a necessity has become entertainment, an opportunity to meet, and a form of collective expression. And the community, united around these new winter games, has begun to identify itself in shared rituals, symbols, and small daily achievements, as well as in the epic feats of explorers and athletes who have fascinated us since the dawn of time, as they still do.

WINTER SPORTS: THEIR HISTORY AND CULTURE

"Snow heroes" are not only strong and resilient athletes, but also symbols of passion and determination. Their exploits—as recounted in books, articles, photographs and then in films—have created a powerful image: snow as a

ATOMIC
Lucas Pinheiro Braathen tests the Redster TR F5 skis
2025

Courtesy Atomic

challenge, a site for adventure, a place of beauty. The adventures of the pioneers of ice and of peaks have inspired generations, igniting a desire to discover, explore, and measure oneself against winter.

Already in the nineteenth century, the first epic feats—from skiing to the ascent of glaciers—opened up a new vision of mountains: no longer solely hostile, but also fascinating, and full of possibilities. An example? Albert Smith. Having climbed Mont Blanc in 1851, he turned that experience into a unique spectacle: his lecture-performances at the Egyptian Hall in London, complete with dioramas, lights, music, and storytelling, transported the audience directly to the ice-bound regions of the Alps. A true multimedia spectacle, well ahead of its time, it had a good two thousand repeat performances, up until 1858, and sparked a "Mont Blanc Mania" among the British, thanks also to marketing strategies that were innovative for the time, with the production of a variety of gadgets and the setting-up of a veritable souvenir shop selling sledges, alpine sticks, and chamois horns, all of which contributed to the British fascination with the Alps as a not-to-be-missed destination.[1]

Great explorations such as that by the Norwegian Fridtjof Nansen, who crossed Greenland in 1888 and recounted his adventure in the book *The First Crossing of Greenland*, also contributed to conveying the fascination of snow and ice as surfaces for adventure: the imaginary and the real begin to merge, thanks also to the epic tales transmitted by books and newspaper articles.

The real turning point? When Norwegian sporting culture met Alpine culture.[2] The encounter between Norwegian skiing and Central European culture was not the result of formal initiatives, but rather of hundreds and thousands of informal and individual contacts. Techniques, products, and attitudes spread thanks to students, technicians, and enthusiasts who took their skis with them on their travels and introduced them to mountain communities.[3] But it is local figures from the steep Alpine landscapes, such as Toni Schruf and Max Kleinoscheg in Austria, Wilhelm Paulcke in Germany, Christof Iselin in Switzerland, François Clercin in France, and Adolfo Hess in Italy, who contributed to the adaptation of skiing to the slopes of the Alps, transforming it from a Scandinavian activity into a modern recreational sport.

In the meantime, everything changed: equipment, clothing, and styles. Rules, federations, and manuals came into being. Among the chief players in the codification of modern skiing, through the medium of the first skiing manuals, were names such as Neumayer, Bilgeri, and Zdarsky. The latter, who can be considered the father of alpine skiing, was among the first to understand that Norwegian equipment was ill-suited to the steep, icy slopes of the Alps and to make fundamental changes such as reducing the length of the ski from three meters to one hundred and eighty centimeters, replacing the two poles with tip discs with a single pole to be used as a scraper. And it is he who was also responsible for the application of steel plates that regulate the movement of the binding and secure the heel for the descent, a binding that would later be perfected by Georg Bilgeri, from whom it takes its name. The Lilienfeld School technique comes into being, in opposition to that established in Scandinavia, known as the Telemark or "free heel" technique, the first of a series of contrasting elements and evolutions in skiing technique. Meanwhile, the movement gained momentum: between 1900 and 1910, clubs and organizations were founded. In Italy, skiing caught on thanks to Adolfo Kind, a Swiss engineer in Turin, who founded the Ski Club Torino in 1901 and then that of Cortina in 1903.

Instructors moved from one town to another, some training thousands of students. Women also began to make their mark, emancipating themselves and taking up competitive skiing. In 1908, Marie Marvingt—wearing trousers and donning skis—demonstrated that skiing was elegant and also suitable for women, helping to redefine the role of women in sport. A pioneer of skiing, Marie Marvingt argued that skiing was suitable for women because it was not "violent" or "brutal" like other contemporary sports,[4] and its fluid and graceful movement made it socially acceptable, helping to create a new image of the "strong-willed," athletic, and independent modern woman.

And then there are the legends. Leo Gasperl for instance, an icon of speed, who in the 1930s and 1940s tackled the flying kilometer, challenging both human and technical limits. His friendship-rivalry with Zeno Colò gave rise to daring experiments such as the Thirring Mantel, an aerodynamic cape designed to reduce air resistance used by the Austrian skier, or the famous Guaina Colò, a lightweight windbreaker made from elastic materials borrowed from women's underwear. These two innovations were developed between the 1930s and 1950s by Colmar, based in Monza, one of the first companies to understand the importance of research and the relationship between the emerging legends of the sport, technological innovation, and communication.

The pursuit of speed would also lead to extreme innovations, borrowing research from fields that were then far-removed from winter sports, such as automotive engineering: this is how the Kneissl fairing was born, a kind of shell to be worn with internal handles. A fairing similar to those used for motorcycles but designed with particular attention to lightness;[5] developed by the Austrian company Kneissl with Egon Schöpf, it was tested in wind tunnels; its cutting-edge shape resembled something out of a science fiction film, but it was real.

And if the Alps were the realm of sprinters, the Himalayas would become the arena for mountaineering. In 1954, the Italian conquest of K2 by Compagnoni and Lacedelli was an epic feat. But it was also a design challenge: their boots, made by La Dolomite in Montebelluna (the epicenter of what would become one of the world's most important industrial districts linked to the sport),[6] introduced innovative ergonomic solutions. Once again, snow, cold, mountains, and extreme feats became a laboratory.

The pioneers, and the entrepreneurs who increasingly turned to them, were not simply athletes or business leaders. They were explorers, visionaries, poets of the ice. Thanks to them, winter ceased to be an interruption, a pause, and became a testing ground and a spectacle, which increasingly fascinated the general public, who over time began not only to watch the exploits but also to want to emulate them, or have a privileged front-row seat to witness the most daring acrobatic feats of others.

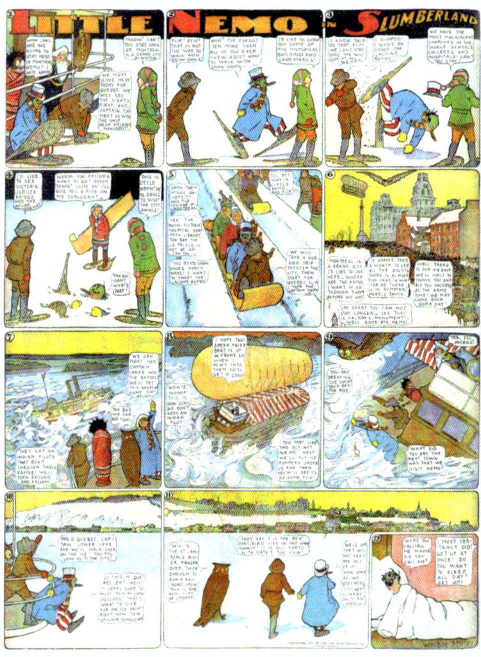

ALEXANDER HENDERSON
The ice palace for the Montreal Winter Carnival
1884

Phototype
Montreal, Musée McCord Stewart

WINSOR MCCAY
Little Nemo in Slumberland
1911

Color lithograph on paper
Private Collection

MOUNTAINS, ARCHITECTURE AND WINTER DESIGN

During the nineteenth century, mountains attracted explorers, scientists, and visitors, attracting an increasingly diverse public: from mountaineers to elegant ladies in search of fresh air. With the beginning of the twentieth century, the passion for snow exploded. After World War II, there was a new change of pace: no longer were mountains simply a physical challenge, but they also became a place of escape, relaxation, and pleasure. Sport retained its central position, but was now woven together with leisure, and a new dream came to the fore: the winter holiday. The first tourist resorts responded to this appetite. St. Moritz was the pioneer. As early as 1856, the Engadiner Kulm hotel promised snow, sun, and skiing in short sleeves. A winning combination. The hotel became the first in Switzerland to have electric lighting (1878), running water, and the telephone. The race for innovation continued: sport facilities, bobsleigh and curling tracks, artificial ice hockey rinks, and summer golf courses replacing the skating rinks.[7]

In Italy, between the 1930s and 1950s, iconic destinations were born; Cervinia, with the Littorina del Cervino—the most modern cable-car of the time—and Sestriere, closely linked to the Agnelli family, which emerged as a model of the modern ski-village with the architectural experiments of Vittorio Bonadè Bottino, and the designs of the Torre hotel in 1932 and the Duchi d'Aosta hotel in 1934, with the invention of the ascending spiral layout of the rooms: off-the-scale architecture with a twentieth-century and metaphysical character set against the irregularity of the surrounding landscape.[8]

The French and Swiss Alps immediately established themselves as glamourous destinations: Chamonix, Megève, Zermatt, Garmisch... names that evoked fresh snow, elegant hotels, and candle-lit dinners after a day of skiing. Nor were the United States to be outdone: in the 1930s, Sun Valley was created, a resort designed specifically to combine sport and luxury. And where there is sport, fashion is never far behind. The slopes became high-flying catwalks, and magazines filled with skiwear by designers such as Lucien Lelong, Vionnet, Schiaparelli, and Hermès. Style glided down the slopes with the same elegance as the skiers, while sportswear began to influence the urban wardrobe. Techwear was no longer simply functional: it became a symbol of modernity, and practicality as well as emancipation. Fashion took its cue from sport to create a new way of dressing – comfortable, dynamic, and decidedly contemporary.[9]

Meanwhile, everything changed with the infrastructure: thanks to chairlifts and cable cars, skiing was no longer hard work, but pure pleasure. You could spend the day on the slopes without having to "earn your way." Winter tourism became a mass phenomenon. The Alpine valleys were transformed into laboratories of modernity, and the mountains inspiration for architects and designers.

Charlotte Perriand, a French designer, captured the spirit of the snow-covered landscape. Her furnishings and shelters were designed to blend in with the environment, using natural materials and clean-cut lines. For her, to experience the mountain does not involve domination but a respect for its equilibrium. "In the mountains, it is only the last ten meters that count, and they are also the most difficult. A very interesting disciplines in all aspects of life,"[10] she said in an interview with journalist Paule Chavasse. And this vision of the mountains, their localities, their people, and their objects influenced not only her own work and aesthetics, but also the design of shelters and ski resorts throughout Europe, from the Italian Alps to the French and Swiss Alps.

Snow and mountains become places where creativity and performance were woven together. Winter became a story to be experienced and seen. From alpine urban planning to panoramic trains, from ski resort uniforms to

restaurants with a view, everything contributed to creating a total experience.
Carlo Mollino, the Turin-born visionary architect and passionate skier (and also ski instructor and president of the F.I.S.I. ski instructors' commission), also helped to define a new aesthetic for the sport and the architecture with a concept based on functionality, elegance, and harmony with nature. Renowned for his alpine architecture, such as the refuge at Plan de Corones where the mountain is not just a backdrop but a living part of the design, Mollino embodied a modern and refined approach to the culture of snow. His passion for winter sports was a deep one, fueled by significant friendships, such as that with Leo Gasperl, whose many exploits he documented.
In 1950, he published *Introduzione al discesismo – Tecnica e stili. Agonismo. Discesa e slalom. Storia–Didattica. Equipaggiamento*, a comprehensive and pioneering guide for post-World War II skiers. With over 200 photographs and 212 drawings, the work did not limit itself to explaining technique, but also celebrated the evolution of the equipment and the constant pursuit of perfection. "For the progress made in downhill skiing we must also thank the techniques and the equipment that have been developed, and are constantly being perfected... Empiricism alone has never led to technical progress,"[11] he wrote, emphasizing the importance of the union between theory and practice, thought and experimentation.
But it was not only through technical manuals and specialist works that winter sports acquired a new key cultural position. A fundamental role was played by visual communication and advertising graphics, media capable of translating the mountain experience into seductive and memorable images. Posters, leaflets, and promotional campaigns became veritable vehicles of dissemination, contributing decisively to the transformation of the practice of skiing into a mass phenomenon.
Illustrators and graphic designers of the caliber of Cassandre, René Gruau, Jean Carlu, Boris Sverdlik, and Antonio Rubino helped create an elegant and iconic aesthetic: clear skies, immaculate snow, stylized skiers and skaters, and inviting chalets. No longer was it the case of promoting tourist destinations, but rather of selling a dream, a way of life, an ideal of beauty, well-being, and conviviality. Alpine destinations thus became real brands, and winter sports increasingly popular at all levels, and among all age-groups.

THE OLYMPIC STAGE: DESIGN, COMMUNICATION AND GLOBAL SPIRIT

In the epic chronicle of snow and sport, the Winter Olympics take center stage. Not just medals and breathtaking competitions, but also culture, creativity, and the collective imagination. From the very first edition in 1924 in Chamonix, the Games have reflected the evolution of society, technology and—why not?—also aesthetic taste.[12]
Like any major global event, the Olympics have also gone through difficult times. During World War II, the Olympic flame was extinguished twice, in 1940 and 1944. The venues had already been chosen—Sapporo, then Garmisch-Partenkirchen, and finally Turin—but everything came to a halt. The flame was once more lit in 1948, with St. Moritz, in a symbolic edition that marked the rebirth of sport and of the whole world.
A truly iconic moment? Cortina d'Ampezzo, 1956. Italy prepared itself and welcomed the world in a picture-postcard setting. There were the first Winter Olympics to be broadcast live on TV across Europe: the sport became entertainment, snow entered people's homes, and Cortina established itself as a symbol of style, elegance, and modernity.[13]
Every Olympics is an opportunity to put on display the identity of the host country, not only through the competitions, but also by means of the colors, shapes, sounds, architecture, mascots, and graphic art. A true explosion of creativity that speaks a universal language.
Take, for example, the visual design forthe 1948 Games in St. Moritz, one of the first examples of integrated communication. Or Franco Rondinelli's posters for Cortina, or Yusaku Kamekura's refined design for Sapporo 1972, in which Japanese aesthetics meet the international style. And then there is the silent queen of the Olympics: the torch. Each edition reinterprets it in its own way. Mario Bellini's design for Turin 2006 was unforgettable, a flame bending in the wind: elegant, light, and technological. Or Philippe Starck's design for Albertville 1992, with its space-age crystal look, and the flame by Studio Carlo Ratti Associati for Milan-Cortina 2026.
And let's not forget the mascots! From Shuss, the funny stylized skier of Grenoble 1968, to Tina and Milo—the two stoats of Milan-Cortina 2026—each mascot disclosing a fragment of local culture. Some won our hearts (such as the endearing cowboy bears Hidy and Howdy in Calgary 1988), others make us smile with their originality. But all of them, in one way or another, become part of the Olympic story.
In short, each edition of the Winter Olympics is a great showcase where sport, technology, design, and communication come together. Athletes become ambassadors, cities are transformed into stage sets, and design becomes the face of a shared dream.
Snow melts, and competitions end. But the memory remains: a torch dancing in the wind, a smiling mascot, a logo that remains etched in the mind. And that sense of global belonging that only the Olympics can convey.

LIGHTS, CAMERA, SKI! CINEMA ON THE SNOW

Winter sports, with their natural spectacle, seemed tailor-made for the big screen. Cinema was able to amplify their appeal, transforming snow into a set and skiers into protagonists of adventures, dreams, and icons. Cinema has played a key role in the imagination associated with snow: it has created myths and settings and evoked images that still accompany us today.
Long before skiing became a global spectacle, there was a figure who had already anticipated the games' scenic potential. This was Leni Riefenstahl, pioneer of "mountain films" and future controversial director, who was the first to grasp the cinematic appeal of snow-capped peaks. In the 1920s, she appeared on the big screen in films such as *The Holy Mountain* and *The White Hell of Pitz Palu*, where the body in motion, snow, and landscape merged into a new visual language.

EMILIO PUCCI
Mosaico
1953

Waterproof printed taffeta
Como, Fondazione Antonio Ratti

Still from Barbarella
1968

Directed by Roger Vadim

In the 1930s, skiing burst into popular culture: races attracted crowds, newspapers celebrated champions, and cinema rode the wave. *White Ecstasy* (1931), starring the legendary Hannes Schneider and a young Riefenstahl, was an international triumph, the pleasure of skiing amplified by the magic of the big screen.

At the same time, fashion fell in love with the mountains. Ski jackets, trousers, and sweaters began to invade shop windows from Berlin to New York, while fashion houses and tourist boards turned to artists such as Franz Lenhart to create elegant Art Deco posters. Skiing was not just a sport: it was style, status, Europeanism. And that appeal transcended the Alpine borders. In Japan, *White Ecstasy* screened for years, while Schneider traveled teaching technique and the disciplines. In Australia and New Zealand, railways and tourist agencies imported instructors from his famous Austrian school, igniting the white dream in the other hemisphere.[14]

The real boom, however, came in the 1950s and 1960s, when skiing holidays became a symbol of glamour. Films set in ski resorts multiplied. Some examples? *Charade* (1963) with Audrey Hepburn and Cary Grant, also set in Megève, and *The Pink Panther* (1963), with Peter Sellers and Claudia Cardinale, where Cortina d'Ampezzo becomes the perfect setting for a mix of intrigue, comedy, and charm. High society, snow, and humor come together, and the mountains become a status symbol.

Even James Bond, the most famous secret agent of the big screen, cannot resist the charm of snow. As early as 1969, in *On Her Majesty's Secret Service*, when we see him hurtling around Mürren on his skis, on the peak of the Schilthorn, the world of 007 intertwines its plots with the wonders of high altitudes. From St. Moritz in *The Spy Who Loved Me* (1977), where the spectacular skiing scenes were directed by Willy Bogner, former champion and master of motion photography, to Cortina d'Ampezzo in *For Your Eyes Only* (1981), with adrenaline-fueled chases on the Olympic ski jump and through the snow-covered streets of the town center, Bond transformed the most beautiful Alpine locations into veritable film sets. We then glide through the mountains of Carinthia in *The Living Daylights* (1987), where Timothy Dalton escapes on the frozen lake of Weissensee, to then skim through the glaciers of Chamonix in *The World Is Not Enough* (1999) with Pierce Brosnan, and return to Switzerland among the peaks of the Engadine. The resorts of Bansko (Bulgaria) and Solden (Austria), the latter appearing in *Spectre* (2015), also become part of the myth with their action-packed slopes shrouded in fog. With 007, snow becomes synonymous with luxury, mystery, and pure adventure. And cinema, once again, transforms the mountains into a dream.

Then there is science fiction, which in the 1960s began to imagine snow-covered landscapes in a futuristic key. The scene from *Barbarella* (1968), with Jane Fonda on a sleigh pulled by an alien creature in a snowy, surreal landscape, is famous. It is the Space Age aesthetic that filters through into ski fashion: designers such as Pierre Cardin and André Courrèges create outfits in technical fabrics with space-age lines. The Moon Boot was born and launched in 1969: with its rounded, futuristic design, it became an icon. Looking like a boot worn by astronauts, it is the perfect footwear for walks on the slopes.

Cinema never limited itself to simply "narrating" mountains: it reinvented them. On the one hand, the glamour of the stars, and on the other, the futuristic fantasy of science fiction. In between, an explosion of style, creativity, and inspiration that has transformed snow into a timeless set. The slopes are no longer simply a place for sport, but iconic settings where glamour and imagination intertwine. Sophia Loren, Brigitte Bardot, Robert Redford, and Jack Nicholson become the stars of memorable scenes set between the slopes and an aperitif in the chalet.[15] Winter

sports thus become fashion, lifestyle, and pop culture.
With the rise of winter tourism and the expansion of mass media in the wake of World War II, snow sports became symbols of status, aspiration, and story-telling. From being a sporting passion to becoming the object of entertainment, winter sports also entered the collective imagination via eroticized, ironic visions, and comics. In the mid-twentieth century, artists such as Pierre Laurent Brenot and René Gontran Ranson portrayed smiling, sensual women on skis or sledges, protagonists of a light-hearted, effervescent, and decidedly flirtatious world. A winter eroticism that blends freedom, beauty, and a spirit of adventure, transforming snow into the ideal backdrop for dreaming (or fantasizing).
And in 1968, perfectly embodying this fusion of entertainment, glamour, and sport, the Lake Geneva Playboy Club came into being. No, it's not in Switzerland. Lake Geneva is a small town in Wisconsin, less than two hours from Chicago. Once frequented by Al Capone, this location also attracted the attention of another famous Chicagoan: Hugh Hefner. It was here that Hefner decided to open his second Playboy Club, a futuristic facility that offered much more than parties with the celebrated Bunny Girls. The resort also provided the opportunity to ski. And so, in the snow-covered Wisconsin countryside, you could alternate skiing on the slopes with glittering evenings with the Bunnies and icons of the American jet set. A mix of sport and seduction that made the club a legendary place, where the American pop dream effortlessly glided between music, snow and champagne.
The fascination with winter sports did not only enchant adults. Children—and readers of all ages—also found the snow to be the perfect terrain for adventure and flights of fancy. In comics, ski slopes, icy surfaces, and snow-covered landscapes became recurring settings, capable of transforming winter into a land of exploits, challenges, and imagination. Since the early twentieth century, the world of snow has crept into cartoons, becoming the ideal backdrop for heroic, comic, or dramatic stories.
As early as 1909, in a Sunday comic strip published on February 7, William Lawler's *Buster Brown* was seen racing through the snow. In the 1930s, science fiction also appropriated winter settings: this was the case with Alex Raymond and Don Moore's *Flash Gordon* in a 1939 adventure, in which snow became the exotic and dangerous landscape of alien worlds. In 1942, it was Walter Molino's turn to bring the action to the mountains in *Pin Focoso*, followed in 1944 by *Captain Marvel*, which also became a paper doll to the delight of its young fans.
In the 1950s, it is*Tintin in Tibet* that marks a turning point. Hergé's adventure, serialized in the *Journal de Tintin* between September 1958 and November 1959, stands out from all the others in the series for its deeply intimate and spiritual tone. It is not just a journey through the snow and the Himalayan heights, but an inner journey made up of loyalty, friendship, and self-discovery. The winter landscape also becomes the setting for lighter, more mundane, and colorful stories. In the 1960s, it is *Katy Keene*, glamourous heroine of American comics, who brings fashion to the snow. In the story *Skating Fashions*, published in issue 57 in January 1961, Katy and Debby show off their elegant skating outfits and *après-ski* gowns, demonstrating how snow can become a catwalk for style. Sport is interlaced with taste, transforming every outing in the snow into a centerfold occasion.
In Italian comics, winter also comes in shades of the noir: in 1967, Diabolik moves through frozen mountains in the episode *La cassaforte del morto* (Dead man's safe), in which the snowy environment contributes to creating an atmosphere of suspense and isolation. While in 1972, an explicit tribute to skiing arrives with *Thoeni—La neve è il suo destino* (Thoeni—snow is his destiny), a biographical story written by Roberto Renzi and illustrated by Sergio Toppi, published in the *Corriere dei Ragazzi* on January 2. Later, as well as more experimental, come the visions of Jacovitti, who sketches out surreal and grotesque mountain scenarios, bringing together skiing, madness, and nonsense in his unmistakable style. Winter sports also feature in mangas with Lynn Okamoto's *Nononono*, in which skiing becomes a journey of personal struggle and identity, aG-DRessing issues such as gender identity, social pressure, and the desire to excel. In the world of video games also, skiing has found a place in iconic games, and in arcades—titles such as *Ice Hockey, Slalom, Ski or Die*, and *Alpine Racer*, as well as more modern and stylized ones such as *Steep* and *Shredders*, which highlight the dynamic aspects and the spectacle of snow sports, helping to spread the passion for the disciplines.
In short, snow-covered mountains are so much more than just a backdrop. They are a shared imaginary world, with a narrative dimension rich in meaning, which has been able to speak to our desires, imagination, and collective memory. A place where adventure, excitement, and pop culture flow like a long, endless ski-slope.

INNOVATION IN WINTER SPORTS: TECHNOLOGY, DESIGN, AND PERFORMANCE

Snow is not only a source of narrative inspiration, but also a testing ground for the boldest experiments in design and engineering. In this field, every small detail counts. Whether it is skis, boots, helmets, or snowboards, technical innovations are designed to improve performance by even a few millimeters or hundredths of a second. In competition, the smallest margin can make the difference between winning and falling behind.
Winter sports have become a crossroads between creativity, research, and performance. Snow has been transformed into a stage in which design and functionality meet at every turn. Italy began to make its mark as early as the 1920s, when Emilio Freyrie founded Sci Freyrie near Como, patenting the first folding skis and antivibration systems. His products were so outstanding in their performance that in 1972, Pietro Albertelli reached 190 km/h in the "flying kilometre." In ski jumping, Bruno Da Col also made history with plywood models featuring ingenious grooves.
With the 1950s, the world of winter sports underwent a profound technological transformation. Skis, for example, gradually abandoned traditional wood in favor of innovative materials such as the lighter and more resistant fiberglass and aluminum. This process would continue in subsequent decades: in the 1980s, titanium and carbon made their ap-

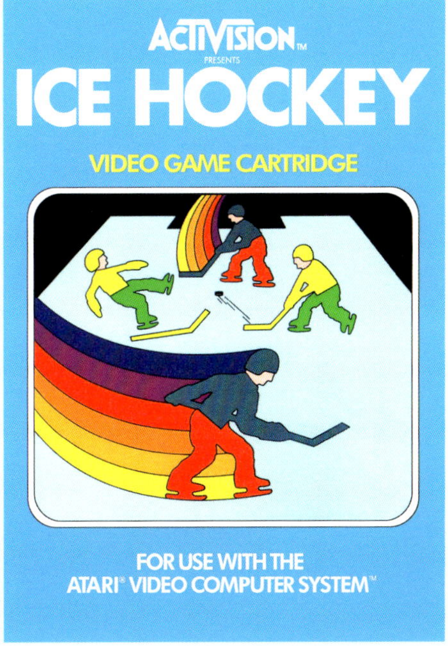

Robert Redford (article in a Japanese magazine)
1966

Color print on paper
Private Collection

ACTIVISION
Ice Hockey
1981

Color print on card
Private Collection

SWATCH
Lauberhorn-Wengen Access Snowpass
2004

Courtesy Swatch

pearance, revolutionizing the maneuverability and precision of the equipment, making the experience on the snow more fluid and more controlled. Ski boots also followed this evolution: they became increasingly ergonomic, adapting to the shape of the foot thanks to thermoforming materials and the adoption of ratchet buckles that improved comfort and safety. No longer is it just a question of performance, but also of well-being for those practicing the sport.

This ferment of innovation did not go unnoticed in the world of industrial design. Some of the biggest names in the industry tackled the challenges of the mountain environment, bringing a new technical and aesthetic perspective to winter equipment. In 1974, for example, Pininfarina designed a range of boots for Garmont; concurrently, Richard Sapper also put his aesthetic vision to the test, reinterpreting the boot according to his own sensibility. Both shared an ambitious goal: to combine form and function, beauty and performance. Winter sports design also won some of the most prestigious awards. As early as 1957, the Compasso d'Oro—Italy's highest honor in the sector of industrial design — was awarded to a ski boot designed by Cesarino Benso Priarollo for La Dolomite-Calzaturificio G. Garbuio. Its rationale highlighted the perfect synthesis of formal simplicity with functionality: waterproof, light, an excellent fit and freedom of movement come together in an iconic product. Ten years later, in 1967, the same manufacturer received another Compasso d'Oro for the 4S boot, admired for its buckle fastening system, equipped with a spring device that improved the elasticity and safety of the footwear, as well as for the overall quality of the product and the harmony of its proportions. In the years that followed, design continued to make its mark. In 1991, the Detector glasses, designed by Renata Fusi, Silvana Mollica, and Paolo Zanotto for Briko, are awarded the prize for "the extreme rigor of their design, which combines the flexibility of the material with functionalityof use." And again, in 2014, MM Design is awarded the Compasso d'Oro for its Masterlite project for Garmont, in recognition of the elegance with which the technical structure was transformed into a decorative element. Throughout all these stages, design has proven to be a key player not only for the aesthetic aspect but also for functionality in winter sports, contributing significantly to improving performance, safety, and the overall experience of mountain enthusiasts.

What we might call the last great innovation—not only in terms of the product—enters the stage in the 1970s and ends up by revolutionizing not only the sport, but also the way we experience winter and snow, profoundly influencing both the aesthetics and the lifestyle of the slopes: the snowboard was born. Its origins date back to the early twentieth century, but the real spark was set off in 1965, when Sherman Poppen, an engineer from Michigan, invented the Snurfer: a rudimentary board made by joining two skis together, designed for "surfing" on snow. It was an instant hit with young people and hundreds of thousands were sold. That simple homemade toy soon became a source of inspiration for an entire generation of pioneers. In 1972, Dimitrije Milovich, inspired by surfing, founded Winterstick, the first company to produce modern boards with foot bindings and advanced materials. But it was in the following decade that the real revolution ignited: Jake Burton Carpenter, with the Burton brand, and Tom Sims, with SIMS Snowboards, competed for the soul of a sport still in search of its identity. While Burton represented the more entrepreneurial side, Sims embodied the rebellious and creative spirit of skateboarding culture.

In the 1980s, snowboarding was viewed with suspicion: many ski resorts banned it, fearing accidents and criticizing the irreverent style of the riders. But the movement grew, gaining ground and popularity thanks to the first competitions such as the 1982 National Snow Surfing Championship (which later became the legendary U.S.

Open), and the spread of specialist magazines that began to report on a new form of snow culture.
The real leap forward came in the early 1990s with the invention of the Pipe Dragon, a machine capable of shaping perfect half-pipes. Freestyle exploded. When snowboarding entered the Olympic Games in Nagano in 1998, everyone was won over by its spectacular tricks. From then on, the disciplines multiplied (slopestyle, big air, snowboard cross), champions such as Shaun White, Chloe Kim, and Ayumu Hirano emerged, and snowboarding became a symbol of a new way of experiencing sport: technical, creative, and expressive.
But the real revolution is also an aesthetic one: pop, flamboyant, and unconventional graphics began to decorate the boards, techwear became an item of streetwear, and snowboarding a direct influence on urban design and style. It is from this context that brands such as IUTER were born, a Milanese company that reinterpreted the visual and cultural language of snowboarding in a metropolitan key, bringing it down from the slopes to the streets, and combining performance and visual identity.
Swatch also made a significant contribution to this landscape. In addition to its well-known collaborations with the art world, the brand linked itself to winter sports with an innovative vision: the POP series introduced features such as the RECCO® system for mountain safety, while the 2005 Access Snowpass combined a watch with a ski pass in a single hi-tech accessory. Swatch also celebrated major events and icons of the snow scene with models such as Fiocco, designed with Deborah Compagnoni, and Swatch The Route, inspired by mountaineer Sam Anthamatten's route up the Matterhorn. This culminated in the Unlimited series, launched in 2019 with skier-artist Nico Vuignier, a perfect example of how sport, design, and visual creativity are able to merge into a single language.
Safety also made great strides: helmets became lighter and lighter but with a high degree of protection, thanks to the use of innovative materials and ergonomic designs. Techwear clothing evolved with the use of advanced fabrics such as Gore-Tex, which is both waterproof and allows the passage of air, offering comfort and high performance in all weather conditions.
At the same time, the world of winter sports made significant progress in terms of inclusivity. Numerous companies and projects dedicated themselves to developing adaptive solutions that allowed athletes with disabilities to fully enjoy the mountain experience. Salomon, for example, promotes the Salomon Adaptive Project, an initiative that aimed to make skiing accessible to all, supporting customised equipment and creating inclusive events.
Among the pioneers of adaptive skiing technology are companies such as Enabling Technologies, founded by Ken La Come after a motorcycle accident. The company has introduced fundamental innovations such as stabilizers, outriggers, and prosthetic skis, contributing to the spread of adaptive skiing on a global scale.
In Austria, Alois Praschberger, a former Paralympic athlete, founded a company specializing in monoskis and snowkarts, which has become a benchmark for technical equipment. In France, Tessier has made a name for itself with a range of products—from dual skis to sit-skis—designed to ensure stability, autonomy, and high performance.
In parallel, the history of Paralympic winter sports has been marked by iconic figures. Among the early protagonists, Sepp Zwicknagl was the first Paralympic champion in alpine skiing at the 1976 Games in Örnsköldsvik. In the years that followed, Austria's Gerd Schönfelder dominated the scene, winning 12 gold and 4 silver medals between 1992 and 2010, thus becoming one of the most successful athletes ever.
The 2000s saw the emergence of athletes such as Sarah Will of the United States, winner of 13 Paralympic medals, and Lauren Woolstencroft of Canada, who won 5 gold medals in 5 events at the 2010 Vancouver Games, Melania Corradini, who won numerous medals at the World Championships and Paralympics, including a silver in the super-G in Vancouver in 2010, Giacomo Bertagnolli, a visually impaired athlete who won 8 Paralympic medals in alpine skiing between Pyeongchang in 2018 and Beijing in 2022, establishing himself as the most decorated Italian Paralympic skier, Marie Bochet, a French athlete and 8-time Paralympic champion in alpine skiing, and Brian McKeever, a blind Canadian cross-country skier who, with 17 Paralympic medals, is one of the most decorated athletes in the history of Nordic skiing. In para-snowboarding, a more recent disciplines, athletes such as Dutchwoman Bibian Mentel-Spee, gold medallist in Sochi 2014 and promoter of the disciplines at international level, have also emerged.
The technical and sporting evolution of adaptive skiing has not only helped to improve performance, but also to make mountains more accessible and inclusive, recognizing and valuing different abilities.

SNOW AS AN INEXHAUSTIBLE SOURCE OF CREATIVITY AND INNOVATION

Snow, with its whiteness and power, continues to be an inexhaustible source of creative inspiration and design challenges. It is not just a natural element, but a real stimulus for innovation, which pervades various fields, from fashion to design, from visual communication to sports technology. In the contemporary world, snow continues to play a leading role in fashion shows, where Moncler and Miu Miu have chosen snow-capped peaks as the setting for their collections. Mountain fashion shows are not solely exhibitions of techwear, but veritable spectacles that combine art, sport, and high fashion, creating an imaginary world that enhances the link between glamour and nature. These events represent the perfect fusion of aesthetic creativity with functional performance, where jackets, down jackets, and snow boots are designed to withstand the most difficult conditions, but at the same time emerge as veritable works of art.
However, it is not only fashion that pays homage to snow. Illustrators, artists, and photographers also continue to pay homage to the mountains and winter sports, capturing the beauty of snow-capped peaks, the tension of motion on snow, and the intensity of the athletic effort. Snow-covered landscapes, immortalized in all their subtlety, have become genuine subjects of aesthetic research, symbols of a world where beauty is as natural as it is artificial. These accolades to snow, ice, and mountains are a testa-

IUTER x Moon Boot
Moon Boot Original Annapurna
2015

Courtesy IUTER

RICCARDO GUASCO x SPORTWEEK MAGAZINE
Milano Cortina 2026
2019

Courtesy Riccardo Guasco

JASMINA KALUDEROVIC
Project for snow footwear developed using AI tools
2025

Courtesy Jasmina Kaluderovic

ment to how nature and culture are inextricably linked in the language of contemporary imagery.
But snow is not only an inspiration for fashion and art: it is also the fertile ground where the greatest designers and engineers compete to create ever increasing high-performance equipment.
There is no end to the desire to innovate. The Delineo studio, with its constant research into form and materials, and designer Jasmina Kaluderovic, with her experiments with AI, are bringing new visions to winter sports design, blending ergonomics, sustainability, and style.
Meanwhile, collaborations between athletes and designers are intensifying to create boards, boots, and accessories suitable for all terrains and styles, from freestyle to freeride. Techwear is becoming increasingly hybrid, with sports fashion and high functionality blending together. Every detail, every small innovation in sportsequipment—whether skis, boots, helmets or snowboards—is the result of continuous research aimed at improving the performance of athletes, often by only a few millimeters or hundredths of a second. The world of winter sports, indeed, knows no limits when it comes to innovation. Every athlete knows that even the slightest improvement can mean the difference between victory and defeat. Designers, therefore, constantly strive to come up with solutions that not only optimize safety and comfort, but also meet the challenge of efficiency.
Winter sports, from entertainment phenomenon to competitive disciplines, continue to be an incredible source of creativity. Snow has become the ideal stage for expressing artistic visions, tackling sporting challenges, and creating cutting-edge products. With each season, new technological horizons open up, while the connection with nature and the mountains remains strong, both in the hearts of athletes and in the collective imagination. Snow, therefore, remains a symbol of innovation, but also of tradition, experimentation and conquest, constantly evolving, ready to embrace new challenges and new forms of creative expression.

[1] A. Audisio, V. Lisino, *Albert Smith. Lo spettacolo del Monte Bianco e altre avventure in vendita*, Edizioni Museomontagna, Turin 2018.
[2] E.J.B. Allen, *Historical Dictionary of Skiing*, Scarecrow Press,Lanham-Toronto-Plymouth 2012, p. 4.
[3] A. Denning, *Skiing into Modernity: A Cultural and Environmental History*, University of California Press, Berkeley 2014, p. 34.
[4] M. Marvingt, *Les femmes et le ski*, in L. Magnus, R. De La Frégeolière,*Les sports d'hiver*, Lafitte Paris 1911, pp. 176-181.
[5] F. Ferrari, *Leo Gasperl. KlSankt Moritz 1932*, Umberto Allemandi & C., Turin-London 1997, p. 31.
[6] V. Durante, *Sportsystem tra fashion e performance. Moda e design, sport e streetstyle, cultura e società nella storia del sistema sportivo italiano*, Danilo Zanetti Editore, Limena 2004.
[7] A. Martini, M. Francesconi, *La moda della vacanza. Luoghi e storie. 1860-1939*, Einaudi, Turin 2021, p. 68.
[8] A. De Rossi,*La costruzione delle Alpi. Il Novecento e il Modernismo alpino (1917-2017)*, Donzelli Editore, Rome 2024, p. 158.
[9] C. Lee-Potter, *Sportswear in Vogue since 1910*, Thames and Hudson, London 1984, p. 20.
[10] P. Nivelle, *Charlotte Perriand. La montagne inspirée*, Éditions Paulsen, Paris 2024, p. 32.
[11] C. Mollino, *Introduction to Downhill Skiing—Technique and Styles. Competitive Skiing. Downhill and Slalom. History—Teaching. Equipment*, Casa Editrice Mediterranea, Rome 1950, p. 24.
[12] M. Osterwalder, *Olympic Games: The Design*, niggli, Salenstein 2019.
[13] A. Denning, *Skiing into Modernity: A Cultural and Environmental History*, University of California Press, Oakland 2015, p. 145.
[14] A. Denning, "Going Downhill? The Industrialisation of Skiing from the 1930s to the 1970s," in P. Strobl, A. Podkalicka, *Leisure Cultures and the Making of Modern Ski Resorts*, Palgrave, Cham 2019, p. 28.
[15] G. le Breton, *The Ultimate Ski Book. Legends, Resorts, Lifestyle & More*, TeNeues, Augsburg 2023, p. 219.

DUTCH MANUFACTURE
Man on skates, with an ample cloak
1625–1675

DUTCH MANUFACTURE
Woman on skates, seen from the back
1625–1675

DUTCH MANUFACTURE
Man on skates, with a large hat
1625–1675

DUTCH MANUFACTURE
Skater
1620–1670

DUTCH MANUFACTURE
Children playing with a sledge
1650–1700

DUTCH MANUFACTURE
Child skating
1650–1700

Earthenware
Rotterdam, Museum Rotterdam

The tiles with the typical blue Delft decoration depict scenes and instants of everyday life during the winter months in seventeenth-century Holland. The tiles were used to decorate the interiors of the homes of wealthy merchants, brightening up the rooms with figures engaged in everyday activities.

HENDRICK AVERCAMP
Enjoying the Ice (detail)
1615–1620

Oil on panel
Amsterdam, Rijksmuseum

This painting depicts a typically Dutch phenomenon: fun on the ice. People are skating, sledging, and playing a game called "kolf," a kind of ice hockey. Avercamp was the first Dutch painter to specialize in winter landscapes. The artist lived most of his life in the city of Kampen. He was deaf and mute, which earned him the nickname "the mute of Kampen."

IT'S SNOWING!

*

UNKNOWN MANUFACTURE
Ice skate
Early twentieth century

Wood, metal, and leather
Montebelluna, Archivio Prodotti Fondazione Sportsystem

Until the early twentieth century, it was still very common to skate on ice using blades attached to a wooden base that was fastened directly to winter shoes with leather or fabric straps. The blade in the image has a serrated tip, which allowed the skater to carry out jumps and spins.

UNKNOWN MANUFACTURE
Footwear for snow
Late nineteenth -early twentieth century

Leather, wood, and metal nails
Montebelluna, Archivio Prodotti Fondazione Sportsystem

To improve grip on steep and snowy surfaces, nineteenth-century snow footwear already featured a system of metal studs. This also slowed down wear and tear on the wooden sole.

UNKNOWN MANUFACTURE
Mountain clog
Late nineteenth -early twentieth century

Leather, wood, and metal nails
Montebelluna, Archivio Prodotti Fondazione Sportsystem

These are basic yet sturdy shoes, used mainly for agricultural work. As in the example illustrated here, recycled materials were often used: note how the upper shoe, and in particular the upper band, is made from the back of another shoe.

ADRIAEN VAN DE VENNE
How well we go together
c. 1635

Oil on panel
Copenhagen, Statens Museum for Kunst

JAMES GILLRAY
Fine Bracing Weather
1808

Engraving with watercolor on paper

JAMES GILLRAY
Elements of Skateing: Attitude! Attitude is every thing
1805

Engraving with watercolor on paper
Chicago, The Art Institute

James Gillray was a famous English caricaturist and printer. He was renowned for his etchings depicting political and social satire, published mainly between 1792 and 1810. Gillray's great flair is evident in his skill in capturing the comic element of each subject.

HENRY RAEBURN
Reverend Robert Walker Skating on Duddingston Loch
c. 1795

Oil on canvas
Edinburgh, National Galleries of Scotland

London Publish'd November 24th 1805 by H. Humphrey 27 St James's

ELEMENTS of SKATEING. —— Attitude! – Attitude is every thing! —

VITTORIO SELLA
Nepal. The summit of Mount Jannu at sunset
1899

Colloid print
Venice, Archivio Fotografico Fondazione Musei Civici di Venezia—Museo Fortuny

Vittorio Sella was a pioneer of high-altitude photography and considered by many the best mountain photographer of the late nineteenth and early twentieth centuries. A skilled mountaineer, Sella opened up several winter routes and undertook expeditions to countries outside Europe, reaching areas that were still unknown, largely uninhabited, and never mapped. His images maintain the perfect compositional balance that he already had in mind before taking the shot. Even when it came to panoramic views using multiple exposures, often in difficult conditions, his patience and psychological tension allowed him to overcome all kinds of complications: the cumbersome and heavy photographic equipment, which was extremely delicate at the time due to the use of 30 × 40 cm photographic plates, the exposure times determined only by memory or with the aid of a stopwatch, the tripod shaking in the wind, the long waits on cold days of endless walking, and the uncomfortable equipment of the time.

ALBERT SMITH, WLLIAM BEVERLY (ILLUSTRATOR)
Mr Albert Smith's Ascent of Mont Blanc in Miniature
1854

A. & S. Joseph Myers & Co., London
Lithographs on paper, and various materials
Private Collection

Peep-show that was part of the extensive merchandising that accompanied Albert Smith's sensational show at the Egyptian Hall in Piccadilly, in which he dramatically recounted his 1851 ascent of Mont Blanc.

ALBERT SMITH, CHARLES WARREN (ILLUSTRATOR)
The New Game of the Ascent of Mont Blanc
1855–1857

Color lithograph on paper
Private Collection

This game takes players from the Egyptian Hall to Tunbridge, Folkstone, and on to Dover, then across the English Channel to Boulogne, Amiens, and Paris (to which eight squares are dedicated, including views of Notre Dame, the Arc de triomphe, and Les invalides). From the French capital, the journey continues to Dijon, Geneva, Martigny, the Great St. Bernard Pass, and Chamonix, with the climb up the Aiguille du Midi, the Bossons and Taconnaz glaciers, the Grands Mulet refuge, the Mur de la Côte, and finally the "summit of Mont Blanc." There is no shortage of fascinating details along the way: "a cup of coffee," "a hot bath," the dungeons of Chillon Castle (complete with prisoner), St. Bernard dogs, and crossing waist-high "soft snow."

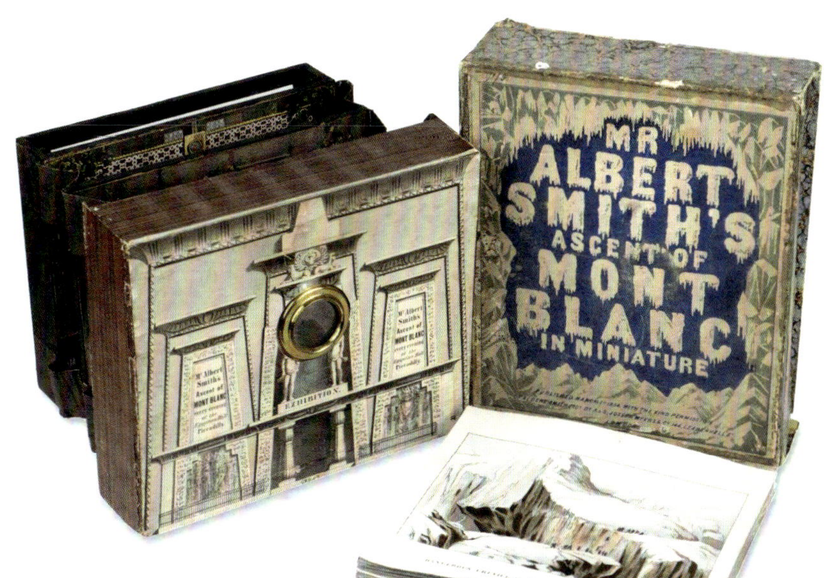

ALBERT SMITH
Fan
c. 1852

Lithograph on paper, wooden slats
Private Collection

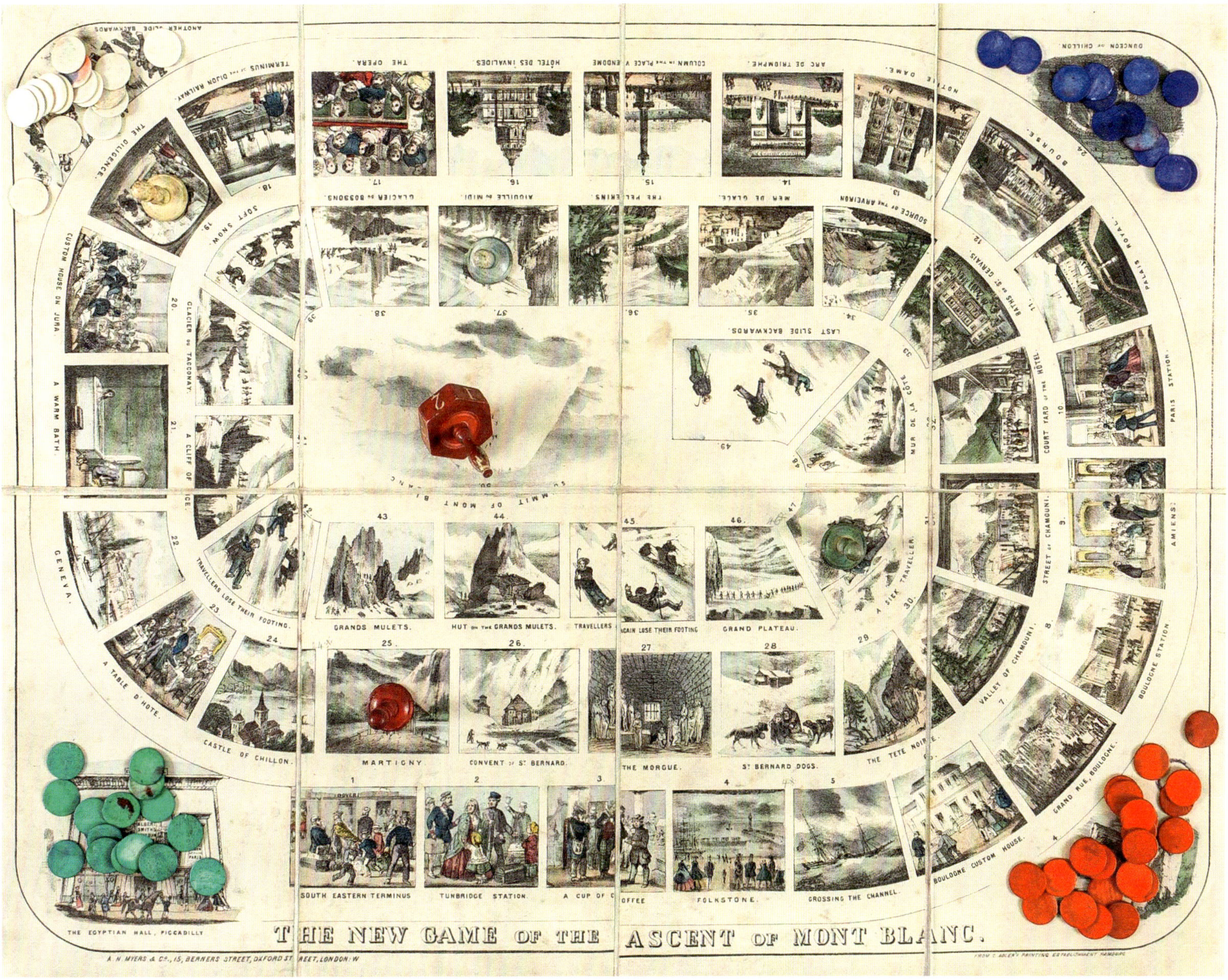

GOODWIN & COMPANY
Curling, from the Games and Sports series
1889

Color lithograph on paper
New York, The Metropolitan Museum of Art

GOODWIN & COMPANY
Snow Shoeing, from the Games and Sports series
1889

Color lithograph on paper
New York, The Metropolitan Museum of Art

GOODWIN & COMPANY
Skating, from the Games and Sports series
1889

Color lithograph on paper
New York, The Metropolitan Museum of Art

The series of *Games and Sport* figurines was published by Goodwin & Company in 1889 to promote Old Judge cigarettes.

JOHN HENRY WALKER
Emblem of the Quebec Curling Club
1868

Print on paper
Montreal, Musée McCord Stewart

JOHN HENRY WALKER
Emblem of the Victoria Skating Club
1850-1885

Print on paper
Montreal, Musée McCord Stewart

JOHN HENRY WALKER
Emblem of the Scottish Curling Club
1850-1885

Print on paper
Montreal, Musée McCord Stewart

JOHN HENRY WALKER
Emblem of the A.S.S.C.
1850-1885

Print on paper
Montreal, Musée McCord Stewart

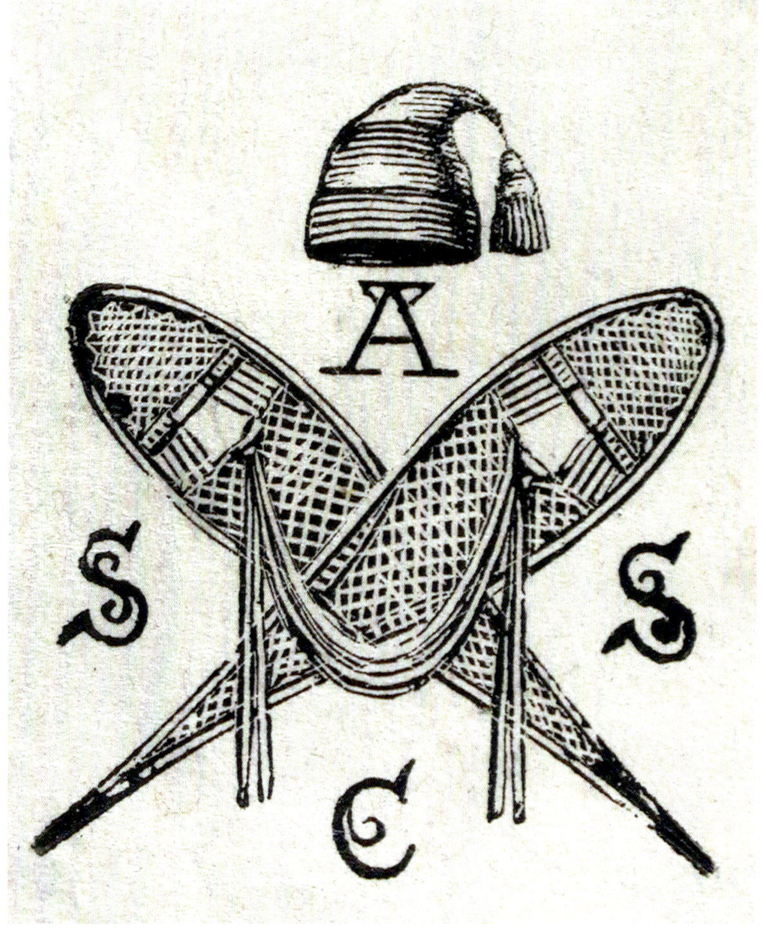

JOHN HENRY WALKER
Emblem of the Snowshoe Club
1850-1885

Print on paper
Montreal, Musée McCord Stewart

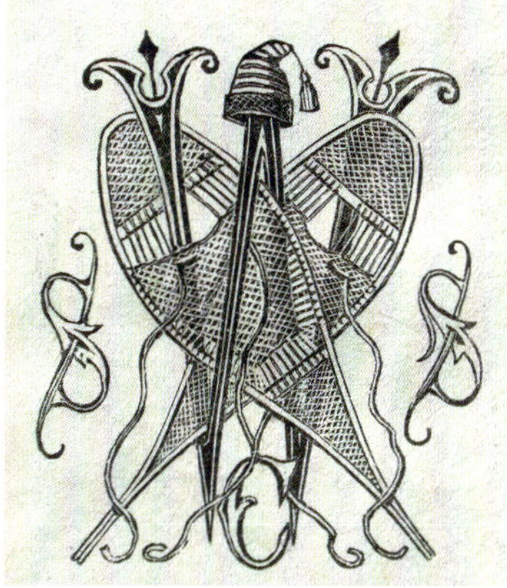

JOHN HENRY WALKER
Emblem of the B.S.S. Club
1850-1885

Print on paper
Montreal, Musée McCord Stewart

WILLIAM NOTMAN STUDIO

Mlle V. Allan and Mme Russell Stephenson playing curling

1876

Silver salt print on card
Montreal, Musée McCord Stewart

Postproduction photograph depicting Mlle V. Allan and Mme Russell Stephenson in a curling scene. What you see is the result of the combining of two photographs taken by William Notman of the two models posing in the studio, and postproduction, with the addition of the background.

NOTMAN & SON

Mlle Allan in winter costume

1881

Silver salt print on card
Montreal, Musée McCord Stewar

BOOTH & FOX
Quilted feather petticoat
1865-1870

Silk, goose down
Sydney, Powerhouse Museum

RAVASI MANUFACTURE
Sledges
1883-1885

Brocade
Como, Fondazione Antonio Ratti

FRENCH MANUFACTURE
Winter sports
1880-1890

Brocade
Como, Fondazione Antonio Ratti

WINSLOW HOMER (AFTER)
Winter—A skating scene, in *Harper's Weekly*, vol. XII
January 25, 1868

Print on paper
New York, The Metropolitan Museum of Art

CANADIAN MANUFACTURE
Tuque Bleue Snowshoe Club uniform
1880–1890

Wool fabric
Montreal, Musée McCord Stewart

The Tuque Bleue Snowshoe Club was a sports association in Montreal, whose name referred to the distinctive blue cap worn by members during snowshoe excursions.

WHISTLER BLACKCOMB [CA] 

UNKNOWN MANUFACTURE
Snowshoes
Early twentieth century

Wood, rope, fabric, and metal rings
Montebelluna, Archivio Prodotti Fondazione Sportsystem

AMERICAN BANK NOTE COMPANY
Montreal Fifth Annual Winter Carnival and Ice Palace Fête
1889

Chromolithograph on paper
Washington D.C., Library of Congress

Advertising poster for the fifth Montreal Winter Carnival, famous for its Ice Palace, the races on snow and ice, and celebrations featuring fireworks and winter sports.

NOTMAN & SON
The Harper Family
1885

Silver salt print on card
Montreal, Musée McCord Stewart

917
Tuque
Bleue
1886-7.

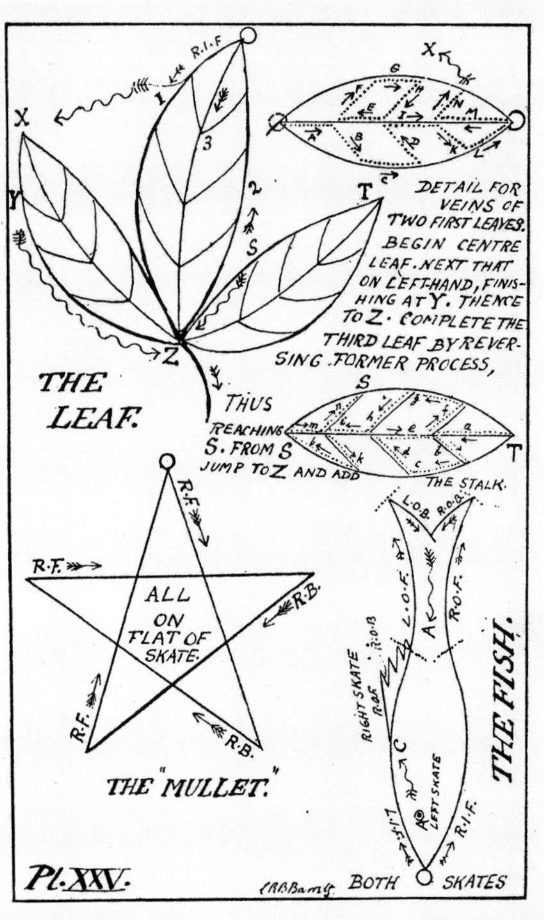

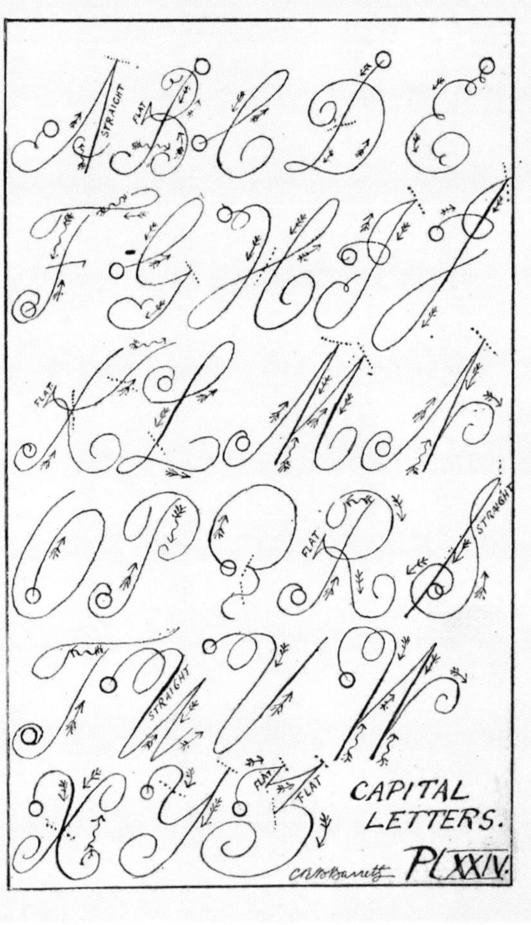

GEORGE A. MEAGHER
Figure and Fancy Skating
1895

Plate XXV
(The Leaf, The Fish, The Star)
Print on paper
Private Collection

GEORGE A. MEAGHER
Figure and Fancy Skating
1895

Plate XXIV
(Capital Letters)
Print on paper
Private Collection

GEORGE A. MEAGHER
Figure and Fancy Skating
1895

Plate XXXIV
(Fancy Figures of Eight)
Print on paper
Private Collection

CONTINUOUS MOVEMENTS FOR ONE SKATE.
DETAIL.
FANCY FIGURES OF EIGHT.
Pl. XXXIV.

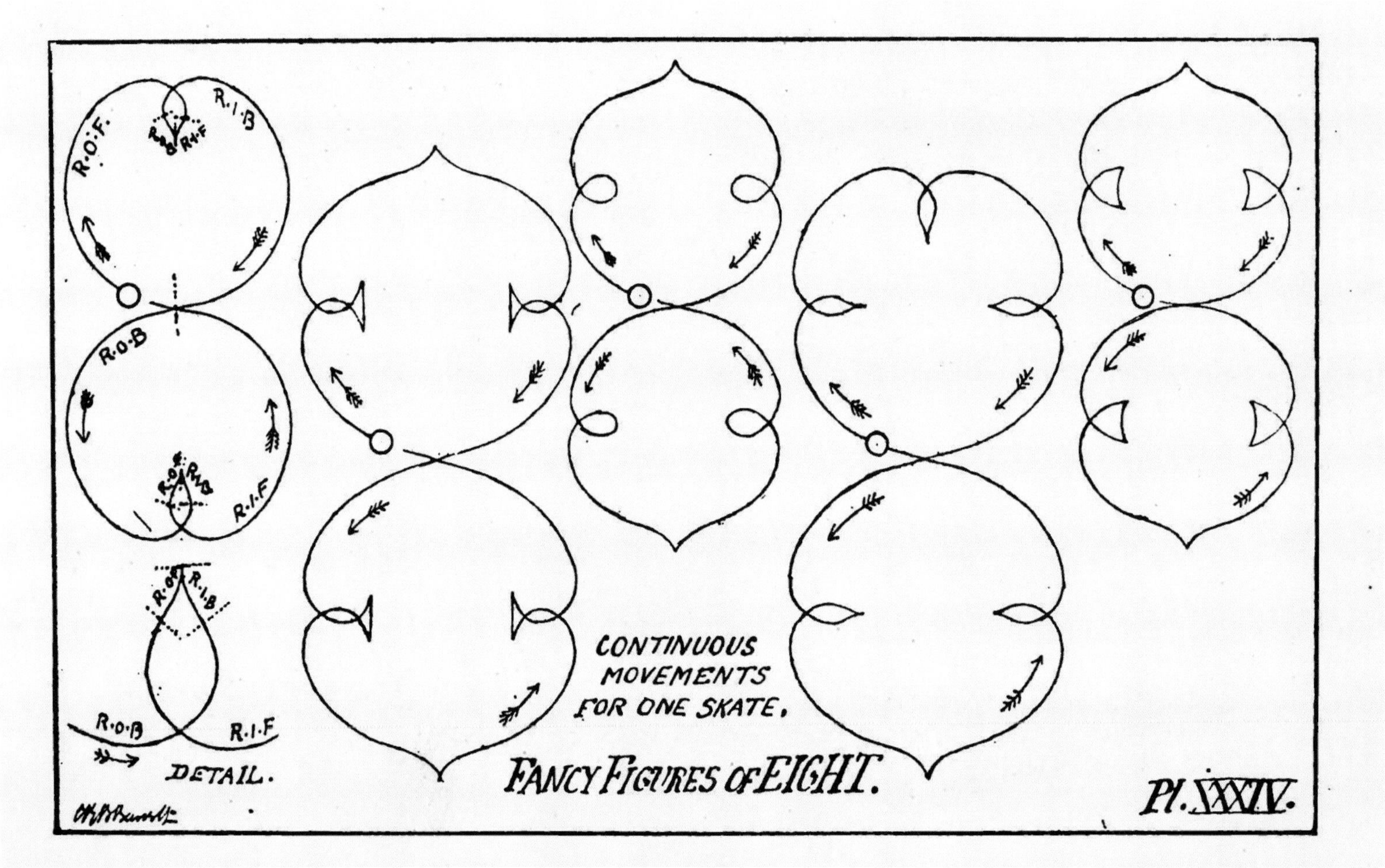

JULES CHÉRET
Palais de Glace
Champs-Élysées
c.1900–1902

Color lithograph on paper
Paris, Musée National du Sport

Jules Chéret is considered the father of the modern poster, revolutionizing urban visual communication with over a thousand advertising posters. His lively, decorative works often celebrate carefree, joyful female figures. The Palais de *Glace—Champs-Élysées* poster depicts an elegant woman skating gracefully and lightly, accompanied by an elegant gentleman in a tailcoat and top hat, symbols of the fashionable Paris of the early twentieth century. With bright colors, flowing lines and a festive atmosphere, the work expresses the dynamism and optimism of the Belle Époque.

Pellegrini

Pellegrini
PHOTOCHROMIE BERN

CARLO PELLEGRINI JR.
Sunday skating
1904-1909

CARLO PELLEGRINI JR.
After skating
1904-1909

Color lithograph on paper
Private Collection

Carlo Pellegrini, known as the "Poet of the Snows," was a painter from a small village in the Como region who became famous for his refined depictions of winter sports. After training at the Brera Academy of Fine Arts in Milan, he specialized in mountain landscape painting. His distinctive subject matter emerged in 1900, when he moved to Switzerland: snow-covered landscapes with skiers became the focus of his work. He portrayed with great elegance the slopes of fashionable resorts such as St. Moritz, Davos, and Adelboden. In addition to paintings, he created posters and postcards. One of his works was awarded the gold medal in a painting competition linked to the 1912 Olympic Games in Stockholm.

ATLOFF & NORMAN (MANUFACTURERS)
Boots
c. 1901-1903

Leather, silk lining, metal
Oslo, Kunstindustrimuseet

This pair of leather boots, with sliding blades, can be transformed into a pair of ice boots.

ANTONIO RUBINO
Cover for Il giornalino della Domenica, *no. 4*
1908

Color lithograph on paper
Private Collection

ANTONIO RUBINO
Cover for Il giornalino della Domenica, *no. 7*
1908

Color lithograph on paper
Private Collection

OTTORINO ANDREINI
Cover for Il giornalino della Domenica, *no. 14*
1911

Color lithograph on paper
Private Collection

STANISŁAW WITKIEWICZ
Boy on ice skates
c. 1890-1910

STANISŁAW WITKIEWICZ
Boy jumping on ice skates
c. 1890-1910

STANISŁAW WITKIEWICZ
Boy on ice skates
c. 1890-1910

Ink and pencil on paper
Warsaw, Muzeum Narodowe w Warszawies

WALTHER KOCH
Internationale Eiswettlaufen. Davos
1908

Color lithograph on paper
Private Collection

CARL BRANDT JR.
Sport-Puzzles
1910–1915

Painted wood, paper, and card
Rotterdam, Museum Rotterdam

BURKHARD MANGOLD
Winter in Davos
c. 1920

Color lithograph on paper
Private Collection

JAN ROTGANS
Ruiter's Schaatsenfabriek Akkrum
c. 1920

Color lithograph on paper
Private Collection

WALTER KOCH
Wintersport
1906

Color lithograph on paper
Private Collection

CARL KUNST
Bilgeri-Ski = Ausrüstung
1910

Color lithograph on paper
Private Collection

MELA KÖHLER
Fashion-plate for winter sports (alpine skiing)
c. 1914

MELA KÖHLER
Fashion-plate for winter sports (sledging)
c. 1914

MELA KÖHLER
Fashion-plate for winter sports (ice skating)
c. 1914

MELA KÖHLER
Fashion-plate for winter sports (sledging)
c. 1914

Color lithographs on card
Boston, Museum of Fine Arts

RENÉ VINCENT
Skater
c. 1920

Pencil and watercolor on paper
Paris, Musée National du Sport

JOYCE DENNYS (ILLUSTRATIONS)
EDMUND GEORGE VALPY KNOX, "EVOE" (TEXTS)
A Winter Sports Alphabet
1926

Color lithograph on paper
Private Collection

The book celebrates winter sports through twenty-six illustrations dedicated to each letter of the alphabet, depicting iconic scenes of these activities, accompanied by playful verses describing their characteristics.

SANDRO VACCHETTI x MANIFATTURA ESSEVI, TURIN
S.O.S.
c. 1935-1940

Ceramic
Rosignano Marittimo, Collezione Raffaello Pernici – Best Ceramics

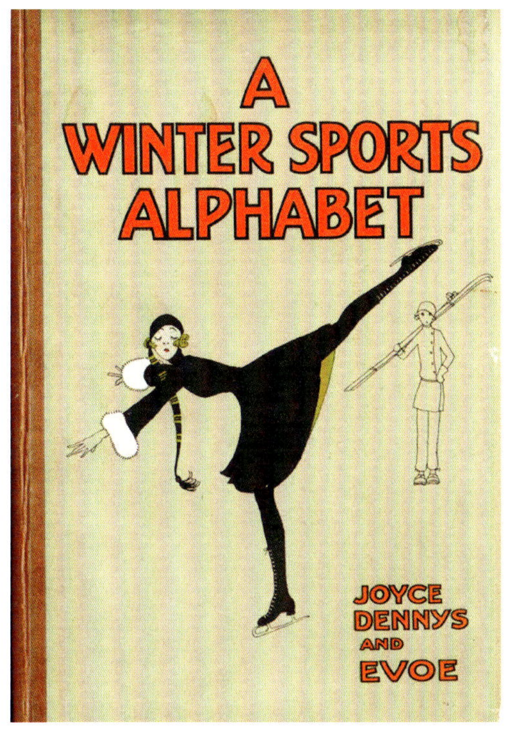
A
WINTER SPORTS
ALPHABET
JOYCE
DENNYS
AND
EVOE

A
A for the Wild Anticipation
(Before we started out, you know)
Of You and Me
About to Ski,
And gazing, Rapt with Admiration
At Vistas of Eternal Snow

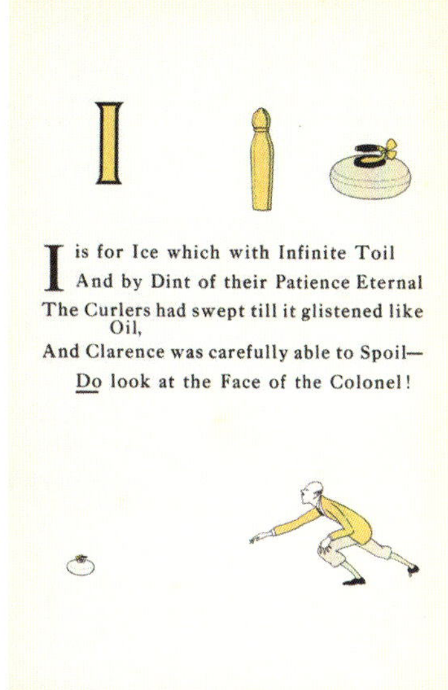
I
I is for Ice which with Infinite Toil
And by Dint of their Patience Eternal
The Curlers had swept till it glistened like Oil,
And Clarence was carefully able to Spoil—
Do look at the Face of the Colonel!

L
L stands for the Luge. Ah! the Labour and Pain!
The Ascent of the Pitiless Slope,
With Plumpness and Beauty and Perfect Disdain!
He could Murder that Thing (but he must not complain),
Sitting there at the End of his Rope!

Z
Z is the Zealot's Slumber
Full filled with Phantoms dim:
Wild memories without Number
The Nerve, the Pep, the Vim,
The Snows, the Alpine lumber,
And All
Jazzed Up
With
HIM.

PAUL ORDNER
Le goal
1925-1930

Pencil and watercolor on paper
Paris, Musée National du Sport

PAUL ORDNER
Présentation de l'équipe
1925-1930

Pencil and watercolor on paper
Paris, Musée National du Sport

AGENZIA ROL
Palais des sports, Mlle Christiane Daumont
c. 1925

Photographic print
Paris, Bibliothèque Nationale de France

WILLIAM NOTMAN STUDIO
McGill University Physical Education School hockey team
1927

Silver salt print on card
Montreal, Musée McCord Stewart

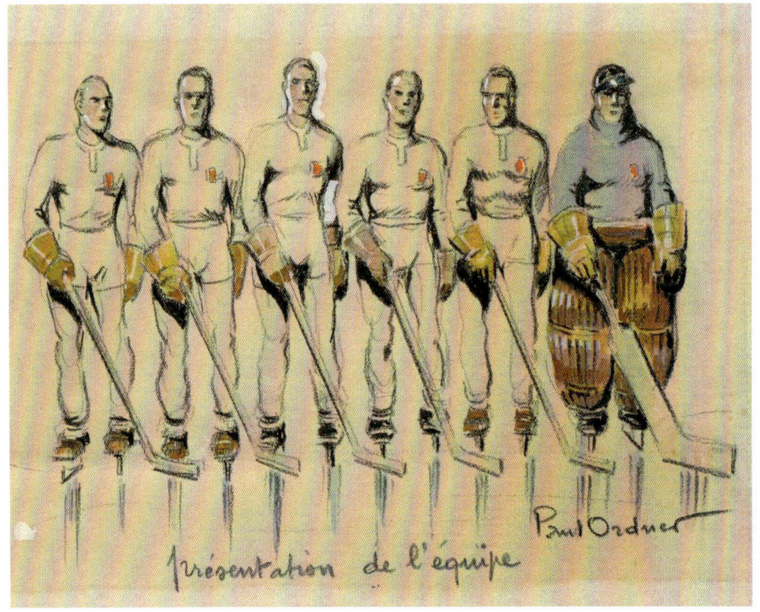

RENÉ VINCENT
Le "shot" le plus dur de sa carrière
1930 circa

Lithograph on paper
Paris, Bibliothèque Nationale de France

UNIDENTIFIED PHOTOGRAPHER
Model in sportswear
c. 1930

Silver salt print on card
Warsaw, Narodowe Archiwum Cyfrowe

HELEN ERNST
Women in winter sportswear
1928

Pastel and watercolor on paper
Berlin, Staatliche Museen zu Berlin, Kunstbibliothek

ERIK HOLMÉN
Model in sportswear
1938

ERIK HOLMÉN
Model in skiwear
1930

ERIK HOLMÉN
Model in sportswear
1931

Silver salt print on card
Stockholm, Nordiska museet

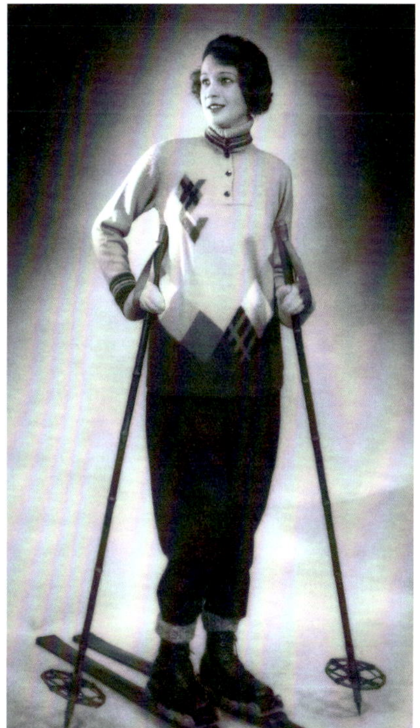

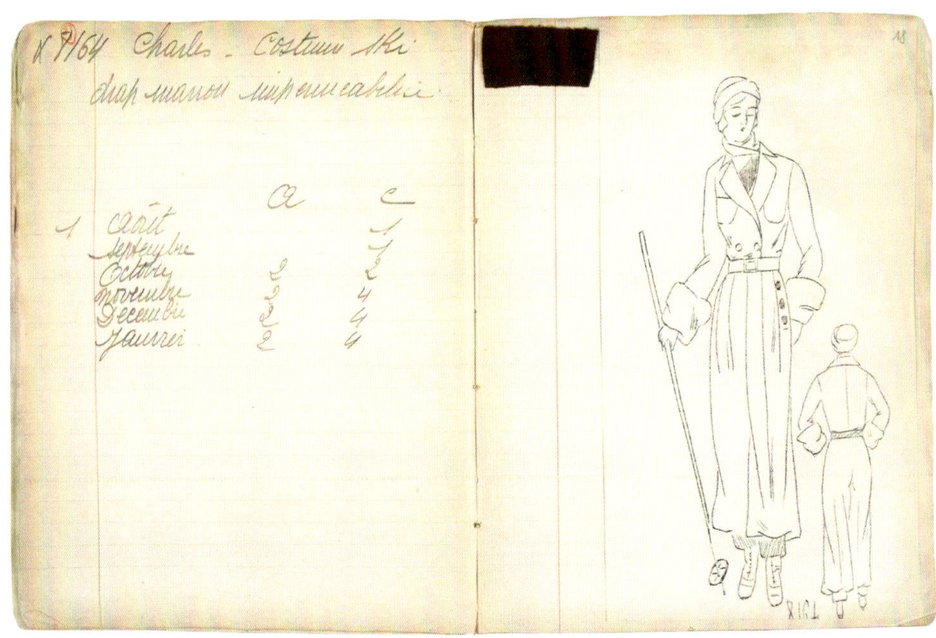

MADELEINE VIONNET
Sketch for brown corduroy ski suit
1933

MADELEINE VIONNET
Sketch for gray corduroy ski suit
1932

MADELEINE VIONNET
Sketch for a ski suit in waterproof brown drap
1930

Ink, pencil, and fabric applied to paper
Paris, Bibliothèque Historique de la Ville de Paris

JEANNE LANVIN
Sketch for a red wool ski suit
1928

Watercolor and pencil on paper
Private Collection

MARCELLO DUDOVICH
Woman skier
1929

Tempera on paper
Milan, Collezione Archivio 900

ELENA SCAVINI x MANIFATTURA LENCI, TURIN
Ai monti!
c.1936

Ceramic
Rosignano Marittimo, Collezione Raffaello Pernici – Best Ceramics

STEPHAN DAKON x WIENER MANUFAKTUR FRIEDRICH GOLDSCHEIDER, VIENNA
Woman Skier
c.1935

Ceramic
Private Collection

STEPHAN DAKON x WIENER MANUFAKTUR FRIEDRICH GOLDSCHEIDER, VIENNA
Woman Skier
c.1935

Ceramic
Private Collection, courtesy of Cambi Casa d'Aste

ELENA SCAVINI x MANIFATTURA LENCI, TURIN
Ai monti!
c.1936

Ceramic
Rosignano Marittimo, Collezione Raffaello Pernici – Best Ceramics

RUSSIAN MANUFACTURE
Woman with skis
c. 1950

Ceramic
Private Collection

UNIDENTIFIED MANUFACTURE
Woman Skier
1935-1940

Ceramic
Private Collection, courtesy of Cambi Casa d'Aste

TAMARA DE LEMPICKA
Saint-Moritz
1929

Oil on canvas
Orléans, Musée des Beaux-Arts

The painting was published on the cover of the Berlin magazine *Die Damen* in December 1929, an elitist image of the modern sportswoman. The title refers to the Swiss resort that had hosted the Winter Olympics the previous year and was advertised as a meeting place for the aristocracy and the film world, chosen by Hollywood stars such as Charlie Chaplin and Gloria Swanson. The model in the painting, identifiable as Ira Perrot, is wearing a sweater by Jean Patou.

ELSA SCHIAPARELLI
Cape
c. 1930

Cotton and silk lining
Oslo, Kunstindustrimuseet

CIMES BLANCHES [IT] 

MADELEINE WALLIS FOR PAQUIN
Télémark
1935

MADELEINE WALLIS FOR PAQUIN
Sestrieres
1935

Watercolor on paper
London, Victoria and Albert Museum

The two sketches are part of a series of 210 designs for the winter 1935–1936, collected in a single volume.

JEAN-CHARLES WORTH
Ski
1927

Ink and watercolor on paper
London, Victoria and Albert Museum

Gray, brown, and blue striped tunic and light blue skirt. The sketch is part of a collection of 136 afternoon and tea dresses for summer 1927, collected in a single volume.

JEAN-CHARLES WORTH
Ski
1928

Ink and watercolor on paper
London, Victoria and Albert Museum

Sports outfit, black skirt, black and white checked jumper, and checked socks. Blue, yellow, and rust-colored scarf. The sketch is one of 91 designs for afternoon and tea dresses for winter 1928–1929 collected in a single volume.

PRODUCTION DENE, NÊHIYAWAK, OR MÉTIS
Coat
1875–1925

Wool, glass beads
Montreal, Musée McCord Stewart

INUIT PRODUCTION
Boot
1865–1930

Sealskin, animal sinew
Montreal, Musée McCord Stewart

INUIT PRODUCTION
Snow goggles
1900–1930

Wood and animal sinew
Montreal, Musée McCord Stewart

INUIT PRODUCTION
Snow goggles
1865–1900

Wood and plant fibres
Montreal, Musée McCord Stewart

ELENA SCAVINI x MANIFATTURA LENCI, TURIN
Maternity in Lapland
1937–1939

Ceramic
Rosignano Marittimo,
Collezione Raffaello Pernici – Best Ceramics

BETWEEN SNOW AND COLORS: WHEN ART DEPICTS WINTER IN MOTION

Massimo Zanella

What happens when snow is not just a landscape, but a stage? When athletic movement becomes a visual narrative and the decorative arts are clothed in winter? The relationship between art and winter sports has its roots in centuries-long depictions that talk to us about much more than simple pastimes: they speak to us of culture, of society, of aesthetics.

The link between art and sport runs through the history of man as a finely drawn but fascinating thread. If painting has always sought to capture the movement and the emotion of athletic action, it is with the advent of winter sports in the nineteenth and twentieth centuries that a new visual and conceptual chapter opened. But the story, in fact, began much earlier. In the Middle Ages, when organized sport was still a distant concept, we already find depictions that express the pleasure of play and competition on snow.

An extraordinary example of a medieval depiction of winter is to be seen on the frescoed walls of Torre Aquila, in the Castello del Buonconsiglio in Trento. Here, in around 1400, Maestro Venceslao created the famous *Cycle of the Months*, a masterpiece of International Gothic art that, with exquisite sensitivity, narrates the rhythms of the year and of human life.[1] The month of January opens onto an enchanted landscape: snow covers the fields and hills, while in the background stands the castle of Stenico,[2] at the time the residence of Prince-Bishop George of Liechtenstein. In the foreground, groups of nobles wrapped in elegant fur-trimmed cloaks challenge one another in a snowball fight, captured in a moment of collective, energetic play that is surprisingly modern. In the background, two hunters make their way through the snow accompanied by their dogs, while a fox and a badger move with caution among the trees, relating—almost by stealth—the silence of life in the snow-bound woods. The January fresco, with its wealth of detail and its skill in blending the courtly with nature and action, offers one of the earliest pictorial testimonies to winter life, not as an allegorical symbol but as a real, lived experience made up of movement, interaction, and connection with the environment.

Among the most fascinating examples of imagined medieval winters are the miniatures in the *Très riches heures du duc de Berry*, the legendary Book of Hours created in the early decades of the fifteenth century by the Limbourg brothers.[3] The page dedicated to the month of February offers a vivid glimpse of a snow-covered landscape populated by figures immersed in the daily life of the cold season: peasants warming themselves by the fire, shepherds wrapped in cloaks. The movements and gestural expressiveness of the figures convey an idea of winter as an active, social time, a time of sharing. With the wealth and variety of their decoration and meticulous attention to detail, the *Très riches heures* offer one of the first figurative representations of winter, anticipating—with courtly elegance—the dialogue between the body and its environment that would return, centuries later, in the paintings of the great artists of northern Europe.

With the arrival of the modern age, between the sixteenth and seventeenth centuries, interest in winter landscapes became more systematic, especially in Dutch and Flemish art. Pieter Bruegel the Elder, with works such as *Hunters in the Snow* (1565), paved the way for a new sensibility.[4] The center of the painting is occupied by three hunters who, together with their hounds, are returning to the village after what was probably an unsuccessful hunt; but it is in the background, which opens as if a theater curtain beyond the hill, that the painting reveals all its narrative wealth: a frozen expanse on which tiny figures move about, engaged in various activities on ice and snow—men skating, children sliding, women carrying bundles of wood, others playing games, diving, falling. A swarm of gesticulations, efforts at maintaining one's balance, of physical encounters and sociability, in which a surprising variety of movements, rhythms, and postures appear. This is not yet sport in the modern sense of the word—there is no codified competitive element—but clearly there are forms of shared physical activity in a communal winter space.[5]

During the seventeenth century, Dutch painting in fact developed a new perspective on the cold season. One of the most outstanding masters who made winter a central subject of their work is Hendrick Avercamp, an attentive and meticulous artist, with the skill to transform ice into a crowded stage teeming with life. In his paintings, frozen

ERNST LUDWIG KIRCHNER
Skating Scene
(detail)

1925

Oil on canvas
Private Collection

canals and lakes become the beating heart of the Dutch winter: men, women, and children move around engaged in skating, trading, playing, falling over, and loving. Snow and ice are not just atmospheric elements, but true narrative agents able to convey the rhythm of cold, festive days. With his ironic gaze and taste for detail, Avercamp captures a world in which everyday gestures become part of a choral narrative, making the winter landscape an autonomous, identifiable genre, deeply rooted in city life and its inhabitants.[6] Winter thus becomes a lived, shared space, observed with a modern eye, able to depict and recount the relationship between body, nature, and society. In the second half of the nineteenth century, the Impressionists also made a fundamental contribution to the evolution of the artist's view of winter. For them, snow was no longer simply a narrative backdrop or a seasonal allegory, but a luminous, vibrant, continually changing material. Artists such as Claude Monet, Alfred Sisley, and Camille Pissarro painted snowy landscapes with light brushstrokes and cool colors, paying close attention to atmospheric effects, nuances of light, and variations in tonalities of white. In their paintings, snow becomes a sensory experience, a field of unalloyed observation. What has changed is the modernity of their gaze: winter is no longer represented as a constructed scene, but as a visual impression, as a phenomenon that envelops, distorts, and transforms.[7] And even though sporting scenes rarely make an appearance, it is precisely this new attention to light, atmosphere, and movement that paves the way for a more dynamic and suggestive representation of the winter environment, anticipating sensibilities that will develop in full in the twentieth century.

THE DECORATIVE ARTS AND WINTER SPORTS

If painting, over the centuries, has depicted winter as a collective scene, a theater of shared emotions and movements, the decorative arts—more quietly, but equally evocative—have also contributed to constructing the visual imagery of winter sports. With the seventeenth century, and with greater intensity in the centuries that followed, snow and activities on ice begin to appear not only in paintings but also in everyday objects: ceramics, engravings, textiles, and miniatures. It is in these details that we find a reflection of a pervasive taste, of a fascination with winter as a time to be experienced and not only contemplated. In the nineteenth century, and especially in the twentieth century, this dialogue between the applied arts and snow culture intensified, finding expression in the idioms of design, fashion, toys, and even home furnishings. This was no longer a simple representation of motion, but its translation into form: winter sports enter the home, in clothing and in objects, becoming an integral part of a modern, elegant, and functional lifestyle.
At the beginning of the twentieth century, at a time when the boundaries between art, design, and craftsmanship were becoming increasingly blurred, we see the emergence of creative synergies between form and function. Emblematic in this sense was the experience of the Wiener Werkstätte, founded in Vienna in 1903 by Koloman Moser, Josef Hoffmann, and Fritz Waerndorfer.[8] Their goal was ambitious: the creation of a "total" work of art (*Gesamtkunstwerk*) that would instill beauty into every aspect of daily life, including leisure and sport. The Wiener Werkstätte devoted a great deal of attention to snow wear, combining elegance with functionality: the garments designed by Eduard Josef Wimmer-Wisgrill or illustrated by Mela Koehler offered fashion of great refinement, with divided skirts, capes, felt hats, and gloves.[9] And it is precisely gloves that in the years that followed became the object of research for Felice "Lizzi" Rix-Ueno (1893-1967), a Viennese designer trained at the Vienna School of Applied Arts and a collaborator of the Werkstätte. Between 1935 and 1944, Lizzi designed embroidered ski gloves, combining the direct visual language of the Viennese school with the delicate aesthetic of Japanese design.[10]

MASTER WENCESLAS
January, from the Cycle of the Months
c. 1390-1400

Fresco
Trento, Castello del Buonconsiglio, Torre Aquila

LIMBOURG BROTHERS
Month of February, in the Très riches heures du duc de Berry
1413-1416

Miniature on parchment
Chantilly, Musée Condé

PIETER BRUEGEL THE ELDER
Hunters in the Snow (detail)
1565

Oil on canvas
Vienna, Kunsthistorischesmuseum

VITTORIO SELLA
Kangchenjunga Glacier
1899

Celluloid prin
Venezia, Archivio Fotografico Fondazione Musei Civici di Venezia - Museo Fortuny

CLAUDE MONET
Snow Scene at Argenteuil (detail)
1875

Oil on canvas
London, The National Gallery

While in Vienna winter sports were synonymous with bourgeois elegance and refinement, in Russia, in the cultural ferment of the early decades of the twentieth century, the decorative arts also became interpreters of the new social and aesthetic ideal. Here, sport—understood as a collective activity and a means for fashioning the socialist individual—took on a central role. Within the constructivist avant-garde, artists such as Varvara Stepanova and Ljubov Popova experimented in the field of textiles and clothing, designing models for a dynamic, efficient society in line with Soviet ideology.[11] Their fabrics, decorated with abstract patterns and rhythmic structures, evoke athletic movement, physical strength, and the energy of the body in action.

Among the most significant demonstrations of early twentieth-century Italian design, Gio Ponti's work for Richard-Ginori[12] represents an emblematic moment in which the decorative arts meet winter sports. Between the end of 1927 and 1928—the year of the second Winter Olympic Games in Saint-Moritz—Ponti designed a series of plates, cups, bowls, and tableware in which skiing, skating, and alpine life became the protagonists of a stylized and modern narrative. The figures, slender, harmonious, often feminine, are captured in motion, drawn with clean, slender lines, in a perfect equilibrium between function and ornament. The snow-covered landscape is reduced to a few graphic elements: pine trees, slopes, and the bare outlines of chalets, which suggest rather than describe the environment.[13] The style, influenced by Art Deco, translates sporting movements into symbols, making each object a small visual manifesto of Alpine modernity. It is not simply decorative: it is a vision of life that takes on form—agile, cultured, luminous—with the capacity to transform the everyday aspects of leisure into an aesthetic experience.[14] Ponti, who had long been fascinated by mountains, also transferred this interest to architecture: in the mid-1930s, he designed the Sporthotel Paradiso al Cevedale (South Tyrol), an elegant alpine hotel nestling in the Martello Valley. Every detail—from the decorated plates to the bright blankets, the striped curtains, and the lamps "that swing with the sound of skis"—was conceived to transform the sporting experience into a "lived" experience of beauty. The hotel thus became a total statement of style, in which landscape, function, and harmony coexisted in a coherent design.

In the Italian decorative arts scene between the two World Wars, the Lenci factory in Turin occupied a prominent place not only for the technical quality of its ceramics but also for its ability to interpret changes in taste and society with grace and modernity. Founded in 1919 by Enrico and Elena König (the name "Lenci" derives from the acronym *Ludus Est Nobis Constanter Industria*), the factory specialized in ceramic figurines and felt dolls with a strong expressive impact.[15] Among its most fascinating productions, a prominent place goes to the famous ceramic sculptures of female skiers: elegantly dressed figurines, captured in dynamic or contemplative poses, often with ski poles and snow boots. These are neither caricatures nor simple toys, but veritable miniature portraits of the ideal modern woman—sporty, independent, and sophisticated. Far removed from masculine athletic rhetoric, Lenci's women skiers express a new urban, worldly femininity in tune with the fashions of the 1920s and 1930s and the Alpine imagery of elite tourism. *Ai monti* (To the mountains), dated 1936, is one of the most iconic examples: soft lines, a pensive gaze, a balance between realistic detail and formal stylization. Lenci's figures thus succeed in bringing winter sports into the spheres of domestic intimacy and art collections.[16]

In the panorama of early twentieth-century Italian decorative arts, Guido Balsamo Stella occupies a fascinating and at times surprising position. Engraver, painter, draftsman, and, above all, an innovator in the field of glass processing, Balsamo Stella was a figure who knew how to combine the essential quality of Central European draftsmanship with the technical excellence of the Vene-

tian tradition. It is from this dialogue that one of his most evocative works was born: the *Coppa degli sciatori* (Skiers' cup), created in the 1930s during his time as artistic director at S.A.L.I.R. (Studio Ars Labor Industrie Riunite) in Venice. It is an object of great refinement, created in engraved, etched glass: on the thin, translucent walls of the cup are disposed the elegant silhouettes of skiers, captured in full motion. The elongated, slender figures move with controlled dynamism, almost dancing the length of the curved lines that evoke snow-covered slopes.[17]
Meanwhile, metal and sculpture also translated the energy of the sport into slender, essential forms. In 1930s Vienna, Josef Lorenzl created light and dynamic figures of skiers, in keeping with the elegance of Art Deco.[18] In 1930, Richard Rohac created the bronze sculpture *Skier*, accentuating the athletic movement with tense, fluid lines. In 1941, Emilio Monti took up the subject with a more compact and measured sculpture, restoring an almost monumental three-dimensional intensity to the sport. Even lace recounted the story: in the tondo designed by Giulio Rosso for the 1928 Venice Biennale, a skier dances alongside fencers and boxers in an embroidered choreographic ensemble of movements and disciplines. It is a poetic, light, and surprising way of bringing the art of movement in sport to even the most fragile of media: filaments and threads.
Alongside painting, graphics, and everyday objects, photography also played a fundamental role in constructing the visual imagery associated with snow and winter sports. In the early decades of the twentieth century, as skiing and skating established themselves as modern and fashionable activities, the camera lens began to explore the body in motion with a new gaze: aesthetic, documentary, but also poetic. Mariano Fortuny,[19] eclectic artist and refined experimenter, captured the rarefied elegance of the mountains as a scenic location, where light sculpts figures and surfaces in a theatrical, white setting. In a dialogue between fashion, setting, and the figure, photography became almost an extension of artistic practice, with the capacity to capture fleeting moments and instill them with mood. A few decades later, but in a completely different register, George Hoyningen-Huene—cosmopolitan photographer and key figure in modernist aesthetics—brought fashion photography to the snow. His images for *Vogue* and *Harper's Bazaar* in the 1930s conveyed a new idea of elegance in sport: models portrayed on the slopes in tailored skiwear, striking poses both constructed and with a studied natural quality.[20]
The white of the snow becomes a neutral background, a luminous canvas against which the body stands out, enhanced by the lines of the clothing and the geometry of the pose. In these images, sport is not action but style: a visual language that combines dynamism and control, glamour and synthesis. Photography, from being a documentary tool, is thus transformed into an avant-garde means of expression.

SPORT, ELITE AND ILLUSTRATED IMAGERY

With the beginning of the twentieth century, winter sports ceased to be merely a physical activity: they became a lifestyle. The earliest Alpine resorts—Saint-Moritz, Davos, Chamonix, Cortina d'Ampezzo—were transformed from quiet mountain villages into elite destinations frequented by aristocrats, entrepreneurs, and artists, the mountains elegantly decked and winter clad with glamour.
This cultural transformation was also reflected in the visual arts, particularly in advertising graphics. Between the 1920s and 1930s, illustrators such as Emil Cardinaux and Erich Hermès created promotional campaigns for the new Alpine ski resorts, transforming the sport into an aesthetic and commercial phenomenon. The snow-covered landscapes no longer depict nature or athletic exploits but become the icons of a sophisticated lifestyle, made up of imposing hotels, impeccable slopes, fashionable techwear, and elegant social occasions.
Emblematic in this sense is the work of Tamara de Lempicka who, in her painting *Saint-Moritz* (1929), depicts a woman skier with a geometric face and a proud gaze: an autonomous, elegant, modern figure, a true style icon, embodying the image of the chic, athletic woman, perfectly at ease in speed as in alpine glamour.[21]
Among the most original and intense visions of winter in early twentieth-century painting is that of Ernst Ludwig Kirchner, a central figure of German Expressionism and co-founder of the Die Brücke group. Kirchner's vision of winter is neither nostalgic nor descriptive in spirit: His gaze is restless, modern, and tense. In the painting *Skating Scene* (c. 1920), the ice is not simply a backdrop but a psychological field: bodies move along forced diagonal lines, poses are tense, faces simplified, and athletic movements become reflections on identity, speed, and solitude.[22]
Fortunato Depero, a native of the Trento area and deeply attached to it, interpreted the subjects of speed, strength, and dynamism within a coherent and personal vision. In his works, skis, mountains, and equipment become elements of a visual language made up of fragmented shapes and vibrant colors, where everything is momentum and rhythm, as in *Montagna con sci e piccozza* (Mountain with skis and ice ax, 1930–1940), a small oil painting in which the peaks are transformed into live geometric structures. However, it was in the 1950s that he produced some of his most accomplished works. Between 1953 and 1956, he designed the so-called Sala Depero in the Palazzo della Provincia Autonoma di Trento, a "total" environment where walls, furnishings, and decorations come together to construct a colorful and dynamic world. Although it was one of his last works, it retains all the visionary energy of optimism, vitality, and invention. In 1956, he also designed the poster *Faites du ski dans les Dolomites*, in which skiing becomes acrobatic, stylized, and light. The figures, cut out as though angular collages, merge with a mountain that evokes both the peaks, and the soaring architecture dear to the Futurists. For Depero, sport was a way of narrating modernity.[23]
In the meantime, specialized publishing grew and in Italy magazines such as *Lo sport fascista*, *La donna*, and *Le vie d'Italia* celebrated snow with illustrated articles that mixed propaganda with modernist imagery. In France, *Adam*, *La Mode chic*, and *Sports d'hiver* dictated the style of holidays in the mountains. In Poland and the United

FELICE RIX-UENO
Embroidered ski glove
1935-1944

Pen and watercolor on paper
Kyoto, The National Museum of Modern Art

RICHARD ROHAC
Skier
c. 1930

Bronze
Private Collection

KAY BOJESEN
Datti and Boje Skiers
c. 1940

Painted wood
Private Collection

States, publications such as *Zima*, *Sport Zimowy*, and *The Illustrated Sporting News* portrayed skiing as a disciplines and a social ritual. Between glossy photographs and stylized drawings, athletic bodies—both male and female—were sculpted into heroic and dynamic poses, consistent with the aesthetics of the time.

While illustrations were a guide to style and behavior for adults, children also had their own snow-clad fantasies, made up of magazines and picture books featuring stories set in the snow, sleigh rides, skiing puppets, and playful sports alphabets. A famous example is *A Winter Sports Alphabet* (1926), illustrated by Joyce Dennys with ironic texts by "Evoe" (E.V. Knox): a snobbish and amusing alphabet that recounts the vices and virtues of alpine life. In Italy, Antonio Rubino, leading illustrator for the *Corriere dei piccoli*, created a poetic universe where snow is play, land of dreams, and stories. Children on sledges, anthropomorphic animals, snowball fights, and Art Nouveau figures populate pages filled with rhythm and imagination. With his decorative and dreamlike style, Rubino transforms athletic movement into visual poetry. His illustrations, often accompanied by rhymes, become bridges connecting play, art, and education. His work extended well beyond the page: many of his images would inspire toys, paper theaters, and cut-out silhouettes. In an era when toys reflected cultural change, winter sports entered children's bedrooms. Made of wood, tin, or papier-mâché, small spring-loaded skiers, sledges, and rocking skaters flooded the European market—Germany, Austria, France, and also northern Italy.

In the 1920s and 1930s, with the boom in middle-class Alpine tourism, winter toys also took on aspects relating to identity and education, with companies such as Lehmann, Fernand Martin, and INGAP producing bobsleighs, ski puppets, and snow-covered theaters. In the 1940s, Kay Bojesen in Denmark created Boje and Datti, two renowned wooden skiers inspired by his own family members.

With the arrival of Barbie, skiing definitively entered the global pop imagination. On the slopes since the 1960s, Barbie, together with Ken, Skipper, and the whole extended family, embodied an idea of sport and femininity that constantly evolved in line with fashion, technology, and aesthetic tastes. An artful mix of plastic, color, and performance, Barbie became a visual narrative, in perfect harmony with the pop language that, in those very years, was beginning to redefine the boundaries between art, consumption, and mass culture.

FROM SPORT TO POP: ART, MARKET, AND THE CONTEMPORARY IMAGINATION

In the same decades that saw games become a mirror of society, the art world also confronted an increasingly visual, commercial, and shared reality. The representation of sport—and winter sports in particular—moved away from the pure celebration of athletic action to become an instrument with which to analyze the body, movement, and the mechanisms of media culture.

It is in this context that we have the emergence of Pop Art, which turned sport into a show-business symbol. Andy Warhol, for example, included sport in his silkscreen cycles—such as the 1977 *Athletes* series—portraying the stars of sport alongside actors and politicians: among these, Rod Gilbert, the famous New York Rangers hockey player, stands out, immortalized in saturated colors and clean-cut lines, in true Warhol style. There is no action in the portrait. It is, rather, a public, glamourous image, an icon in which the athlete becomes a brand and the body a pop surface to be collected.

In the years that followed, pop language continued in its dialogue with winter sports, also extending to everyday objects, of which an emblematic example is the collection created by Bomber Skis in a limited edition in 2015 and decorated with the works of Keith Haring and Jean-Michel Basquiat, on high-performance skis produced in

Italy and sold at the Gagosian Shop on Madison Avenue for over $2,500. These were symbols of the full integration of contemporary art and the luxury market, on which Haring's essential figures and Basquiat's nervous lines become dynamic patterns, conceived for the snow but also to be exhibited. Art, from being an object to be contemplated, is transformed into an object to be used, collected, and consumed. This is Warhol's vision come true: Art is a repeatable, serial visual system, fully integrated into the economy of the image.

This reflection on the spectacularization of sport opens up new avenues of cross-fertilization between art, design, and visual communication. In Italy, one artist who was able to translate these themes with a personal style is Ugo Nespolo, who, with his unmistakable ironic and colorful style, repeatedly depicted winter sports and transformed them into lively and accessible graphic compositions. His language, influenced by cinema, advertising, and pop culture, restores a collective, communicative dimension to the sport, able to unite form with narrative.[24]

This dialogue between art and sport is also reflected in collaborations with the world of design. The Swatch brand, for example, launched special edition watches inspired by snow, designed by illustrators such as Ted Scapa, whose light and colorful graphics celebrate the more playful side of winter. In 2023, the Swiss freerider Nico Vuignier collaborated with the Chilean artist Gabriel Ebensberger—aka C'EST BIEN NILS—on a Swatch X You collection inspired by the Crans-Montana freestyle park, with designs referencing digital languages and meme culture. Since the 1990s, the world of snowboarding has also proved to be a privileged space for visual experimentation with boards designed not only for their technical performance but also as graphic surfaces hosting a wide variety of styles and languages. Burton, for example, one of the most active brands, produced iconic graphics with the Balance series (2000) decorated by Mike Parillo, the Ouija model (1994), and the controversial Love Series of 2008–2009. Other examples include Jeff Brushie's Brushie Trout (1993), Terje Haakonsen's Haakon Air (1994), and Michi Albin's board (2002) decorated by Mark Gonzales.

Lib Tech consolidated its strong visual identity with Jamie Lynn's pro models, including the famous Whales (1994–1995), and collaborations with Matt Cummins. Brands such as Sims, K2, Forum, and A Snowboards have defined the graphic imagery of freestyle snowboarding thanks to figures such as Peter Line, Noah Salasnek, Travis Parker, and David Vincent.

A number of collaborations crossed the boundaries of sport and moved into art and design, including the collaboration between Jeff Koons and Burton in 2016, and Caia Koopman and Rossignol in 2013, which brought pop, street, and surrealist aesthetics to the slopes.

In more recent years, the dialogue has continued with the new generations of visual artists. Burton has collaborated with creatives such as Brendan Monroe, Nani Chacon, and Scott Lenhardt; Jones Snowboards has turned to illustrators such as Annie Brace and Joseph Toney; and Arbor has involved Samborghini, known for his airbrush approach and pop iconography. From historic Pop Art to contemporary graphic experimentation, industrial design, skate culture, and digital languages, winter sports confirm their place as an ever-changing expressive space.

Surfaces alter and formats multiply, but the visual potential of the body in motion on snow remains intact: a powerful, recognizable image capable of crossing the boundaries between art, technique, and culture.

ANTONIO RUBINO
Fascino della neve
1949

Color lithograph on paper
Private Collection

FORTUNATO DEPERO
Dolomiti e Sci
1956

Color lithograph on paper
Private Collection

ANDY WARHOL
Rod Gilbert
1977

Color silkscreen print on canvas
Private Collection

VICTOR VASARELY
Skier
1984

Color silkscreen print on paper
Private Collection

GRIFFIN SIEBERT x NITRO
Nitro Mercy Women's Snowboard
2025

Wood, plastic materials, and paint
Private Collection

[1] E. Castelnuovo, *I mesi di Trento: gli affreschi di torre Aquila e il gotico internazionale*, TEMI per Casa di Risparmio di Trento, Trento 1986.
[2] It was Nicolò Rasmo who in the 1960s identified the castle of Stenico in the January fresco; see N. Rasmo, *Gli affreschi di Torre Aquila a Trento*, Manfrini, Trento 1975.
[3] L. Ferri, H. Jacquemard, *Les Très riches heures du duc de Berry: Un livre-cathédrale*, Skira-Domaine de Chantilly, Paris-Chantilly 2018.
[4] N.M. Orenstein (edited by), *Pieter Bruegel the Elder: drawings and prints*, The Metropolitan Museum of Art-Yale University Press, New York-New Haven-London 2001.
[5] C. Bischoff, *Kunsthistorisches Museum Vienna*, Hannibal, Veurne 2010.
[6] J. Blanc, *Il Secolo d'oro olandese*, Einaudi, Milan 2025.
[7] *Gli impressionisti e la neve. La Francia e l'Europa*, exhibition catalogue edited by M. Goldin (Turin, Promotrice delle Belle Arti, November 27, 2004-April 25, 2005), Silvana Editoriale, Cinisello Balsamo 2004.
[8] V. Terraroli (edited by), *Ver Sacrum. La rivista della Secessione Viennese 1898-1903*, Skira, Milan 2018.
[9] R. Stern, *Against Fashion: Clothingas Art, 1850-1930*, MIT Press, Cambridge 2004.
[10] *Felice [Lizzi] Rix-Ueno: Design Fantasy Originating in Vienna*, exhibition catalogue (Kyoto, The National Museum of Modern Art, November 16, 2021-January 16, 2022), The National Museum of Modern Art, Kyoto, 2021.
[11] *Amazzoni dell'Avanguardia*, exhibition catalogue edited by J.E. Bowlt and M. Drutt (Venice, Peggy Guggenheim Collection, March 1-May 28, 2000), Guggenheim Museum, Venice-New York 2000.
[12] V. Terraroli, *Dizionario Skira delle arti decorative moderne 1851-1942*, Skira, Milan 2001; *Gio Ponti. Ceramiche/Ceramics 1922-1967*, exhibition catalogue edited by C. Casali and S. Cretella (Faenza, MIC, March 17-October 13, 2024), Dario Cimorelli Editore, Milan 2024.
[13] L. Frescobaldi Malenchini, M.T. Giovannini, O. Rucellai (edited by), *Gio Ponti. La collezione del Museo Richard-Ginori della Manifattura di Doccia*, Maretti Editore, Bologna 2015.
[14] *Art Déco. Il trionfo della modernità*, exhibition catalogue edited by V. Terraroli (Milan, Palazzo Reale, February 27-June 29, 2025), 24 ORE Cultura, Milan 2025; *Art Déco. Gli anni ruggenti in Italia 1919-1930*, exhibition catalogue edited by V. Terraroli (Forlì, Musei San Domenico, February 11-June 18, 2017), Silvana Editoriale, Cinisello Balsamo 2017.
[15] V. Linfante, *Il giocattolo italiano nella prima metà del Novecento*, 24 ORE Cultura, Milan 2013.
[16] *Lenci. Le ceramiche della collezione Giuseppe e Gabriella Ferrero*, exhibition catalogue edited by C. Casali and V. Terraroli (Faenza, MIC, March 4-June 3, 2018), Silvana Editoriale, Cinisello Balsamo 2018; E. Pagella, V. Terraroli (edited by), *Lenci. Sculture in ceramica 1927-1937*. Allemandi, Turin 2010.
[17] M. Heiremans *SALIR: Studio Ars et Labor Industrie Riunite; Contemporary Glass-Decorating on Murano, 1923-1993*, Arnoldsche, Stuttgart 2024.
[18] M. Zanella, "Art Déco: el gusto de los 'années folles' entre diseño, arte y glamour," in *Tamara de Lempicka. Queen of Art Deco*, exhibition catalogue edited by G. Mori (Madrid, October 5, 2018-February 24, 2019), Arthemisia Books, Rome 2018; M. Zanella, *I maestri dell'architettura: Déco*, Hachette Fascicoli, Milan 2012; R. Bossaglia, "Che cos'è il Déco," in R. Bossaglia, V. Terraroli (edited by), *Milan Déco. La fisionomia della città negli anni Venti*, Skira, Milan 1999.
[19] *I Fortuny. Una storia di famiglia*, exhibition catalogue edited by D. Ferretti and C. Da Roit (Venice, Fortuny Museum, May 11-November 13, 2019), Fondazione Musei Civici di Venezia, Venice 2019.
[20] *George Hoyningen-Huene. Glamour and Avant-Garde*, exhibition catalogue edited by S. Brown (Milan, Palazzo Reale, January 21-May 18, 2025), Moebius, Milan 2025.
[21] *Tamara de Lempicka*, exhibition catalogue edited by G. Mori and F. Rinaldi (San Francisco, Fine Arts Museum, October 12, 2024-February 9, 2025), Fine Art Museum San Francisco-Yale University Press, San Francisco-New Haven-London 2024; G. Mori, *Tamara de Lempicka*, exhibition catalogue (Turin, Sale Chiablese, March 19-August 30, 2015), 24 ORE Cultura, Milan 2015.
[22] *Da Kirchner a Nolde. Espressionismo tedesco 1905-1913* exhibition catalogue edited by M.M. Moeller and S. Zuffi (Genoa, Palazzo Ducale, March 5-July 12, 2015), Skira, Milan 2015.
[23] *Depero. Cavalcata fantastica*, exhibition catalogue edited by S. Risaliti and E. Francioli (Florence, Palazzo Medici Riccardi, September 28, 2023-January 28, 2024), Officina Libraria, Rome 2023.
[24] *Universo Nespolo*, exhibition catalogue edited by S. Parmiggiani (Verbania, Villa Giulia, May 17-September 29, 2025), Moebius, Milan 2025.

Sironi

MARIO SIRONI
Hockey
c.1924

Tempera and pencil on paper
Private Collection, courtesy of Il Ponte Casa d'Aste

The composition is probably the initial idea for the illustration published in La Rivista Illustrata del Popolo d'Italia *in March 1924.*

LILL TSCHUDI
Ice hockey
1933

Color linocut on paper
Private Collection

An abstract composition capturing the dynamism of ice hockey players, whose movements are linked by the sinuous, rhythmic lines of their skates. Using only three blocks, Tschudi creates a vibrant, moving image that represents her interest in the vital, physical rhythms of everyday life. The print was exhibited at the Fourth Exhibition of British Linocuts in 1933.

LILL TSCHUDI
Sledging
1931

Color linocut on paper
Private Collection

LILL TSCHUDI
Siesta
(Ortstockhaus refuge in Braunwald)
1939

Three-color linocut on paper
Private Collection

DAR'IA NIKOLAEVNA PREOBRAZHENSKAIA x GREAT IVANOVO-VOZNESENSK TEXTILE MILL
Skiers
c. 1930

DAR'IA NIKOLAEVNA PREOBRAZHENSKAIA x GREAT IVANOVO-VOZNESENSK TEXTILE MILL
Skiers
c. 1930

DAR'IA NIKOLAEVNA PREOBRAZHENSKAIA x GREAT IVANOVO-VOZNESENSK TEXTILE MILL
Ice Skaters
c. 1930

Printed fabric
St. Petersburg, Russian State Museum

STEFAN OSIECKI
Illustration for the cover of the magazine Zima, *no. 2*
1929

Print on paper
Krakow, Biblioteka Jagiellońska

The Polish magazine Zima *was entirely dedicated to winter sports and tourism, documenting the activities and ski resorts of Poland and Central Europe in the 1930s.*

ZIMA
NR. 2
OSIECKI-29

GUIDO BALSAMO STELLA x S.A.L.I.R., MURANO
Vase with skiers
1929–1930

Engraved glass
Private Collection, courtesy Aste Boetto

The surface of the vase is engraved with iconic figures of male and female skiers, without any attempt at perspective, set among mountain slopes and stylized snowflakes. The vase was engraved on the wheel by Franz Pelzel, who had been working with Balsamo Stella since the 1920s.

GUIDO BALSAMO STELLA
Drawings for the Vase with Skiers
c. 1929

Pencil on tracing paper
Venice, Archivio S.A.L.I.R., Centro Studi del Vetro, Istituto di Storia dell'Arte, Fondazione Giorgio Cini

UNKNOWN AUTHOR
Advertisement for Freyrie skis, in Rivista mensile del CAI, *no. 50*
October 1931

UNKNOWN AUTHOR
Advertisement for Freyrie folding skis
c. 1930

Print on paper
Archivio Freyrie

PIERO BERNARDINI
Freyrie folding ski
1929

Lithograph on card
Archivio Freyrie

Advertising poster created for the Freyrie company. The poster features a stylized female figure on the snow with folding skis and reproduces the company's first logo, designed in 1927 on behalf of Emilio Freyrie, the company's founder, for the launch of the new folding models.

WOOLRICH
Men's ski suit: jacket and trousers
Women's ski suit: jacket with inner waistcoat and trousers
c. 1930

Massa Lombarda, Archivi Mazzini

COURCHEVEL [FR] 

SANDRO VACCHETTI x MANIFATTURA ESSEVI, TURIN
Sci sci
c. 1935-1940

Ceramic
Rosignano Marittimo, Collezione Raffaello Pernici - Best Ceramics

TARCISIO TOSIN x MANIFATTURA LA FRECCIA, VICENZA
Skiing woman (snowplough)
c. 1940

Ceramic
Rosignano Marittimo, Collezione Raffaello Pernici - Best Ceramics

RENÉ VINCENT
The little skier, and her friend dragging the sledge
c. 1920-1930

Pencil on paper
Paris, Musée National du Sport

TARCISIO TOSIN
Skier
c. 1940-1950

Ceramic
Rosignano Marittimo, Collezione Raffaello Pernici - Best Ceramics

MANIFATTURA LENCI, TURIN
Injured skier
c. 1930

Ceramic
Rosignano Marittimo, Collezione Raffaello Pernici - Best Ceramics

TARCISIO TOSIN
Skier with skis on her shoulder
c. 1940-1950

Ceramic
Rosignano Marittimo, Collezione Raffaello Pernici - Best Ceramics

ELENA SCAVINI x MANIFATTURA LENCI, TURIN
Skier
c. 1930

Ceramic
Rosignano Marittimo, Collezione Raffaello Pernici - Best Ceramics

LOTHAR RÜBELT
FIS races in Innsbruck
1933

Silver salt print on card
Vienna, Österreichische Nationalbibliothek

UNKNOWN MANUFACTURE
Straw overshoe
Early twentieth century

Wood, bracts and wire
Montebelluna, Archivio Prodotti Fondazione Sportsystem

Cover of the magazine Sapere
January 1938

Color lithograph on paper
Private Collection

PHOTOGRAPHER UNKNOWN
Leo Gasperl
1931

Silver salt print on card
Private Collection

Leo Gasperl attempting to set an alpine skiing record in Kitzbühel in 1931, wearing a helmet and aerodynamic protective shield.

VIVIAN CAULFIELD
How to Ski
1913

Bronson Tweed Publishing, London
Private Collection

VIVIAN CAULFIELD
Ski-ing Turns
1924

Nisbet & Co., London
Private Collection

DRAGO ULAGA
Smučanje
c.1955

Državna založba Slovenije, Ljubljana
Private Collection

EMMA BORMANN
Das Skibuch
1922

Gesellschaft für vervielfältigende Kunst, Vienna
Private Collection

LEO GASPERL
Scuola di Sci. Discesismo
1939

Ulrico Hoepli Editore, Milan
Private Collection

CARLO MOLLINO
Introduzione al discesismo
1950

Casa Editrice Mediterranea, Rome
Private Collection

ROBERT KUMP
Smučanje
1931

Državna založba Slovenije, Ljubljana
Private Collection

CLIF TAYLOR
Ski in a day!
1964

Grosset & Dunlap, New York
Private Collection

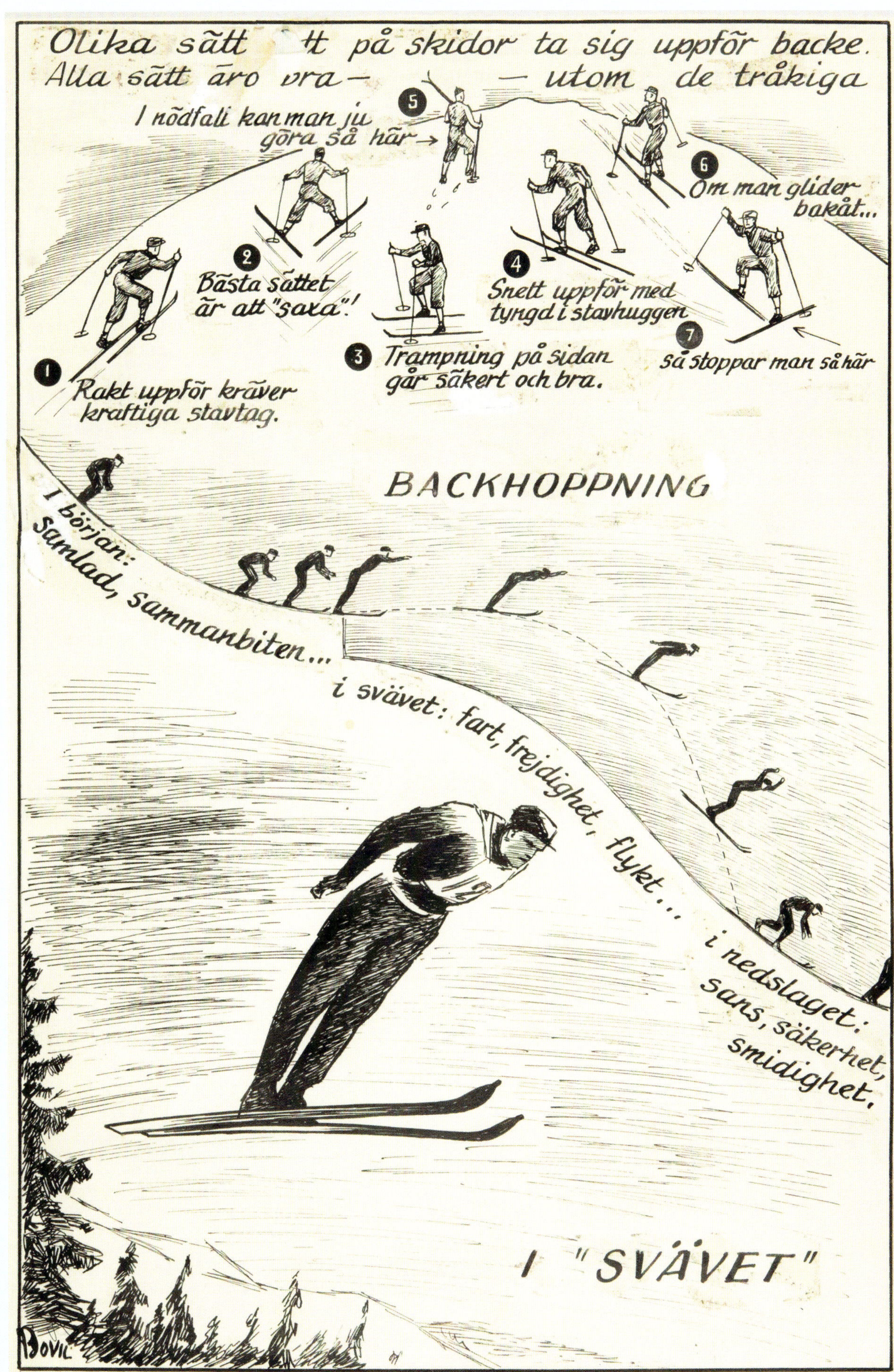

BO VILSON (BOVIL)
Illustration for skiers
1940–1945

Woodcut on paper
Värmlands, Värmlands Museum

The upper part of the image illustrates seven different techniques for ascending a ski slope. The second half of the image illustrates ski jumping, from the beginning to the jump and the landing. Next to the illustration is a caption that describes in detail the jump that appears in the foreground.

Salpaus bindings set
c. 1960

Silkscreen print on card
Turku, Turun kaupunginmuseo

Instructions for lubricating Rex skis
c. 1960

Silkscreen print on card
Turku, Turun kaupunginmuseo

Suksiside-Bindningen bindings set
c. 1950

Silkscreen print on card
Turku, Turun kaupunginmuseo

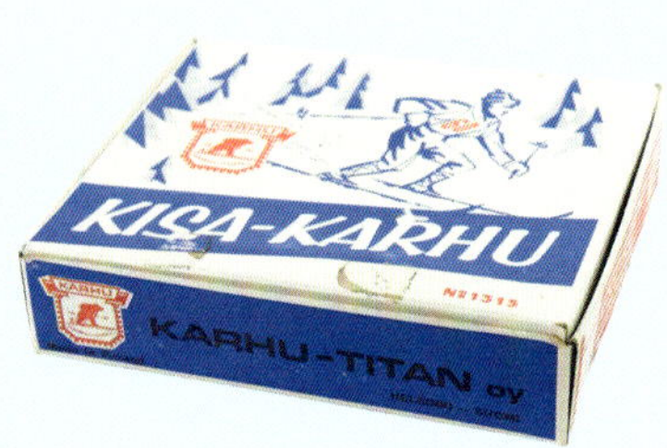

Kisa-Karhu bindings set
1950–1960

Silkscreen print on card
Turku, Turun kaupunginmuseo

Kiva ski wax pack
1930

Silkscreen print on aluminum
Helsinki, Helsingin kaupunginmuseo

Veli ski wax box
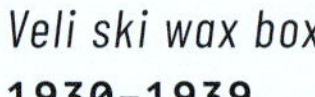
1930–1939

Silkscreen print on aluminum
Helsinki, Helsingin kaupunginmuseo

Rotanloukku bindings set
1935–1940

Silkscreen print on card
Helsinki, Helsingin kaupunginmuseo

Voitto Junior ski bindings set
c. 1950

Various materials
Turku, Turun kaupunginmuseo

FRANZ LENHART
Nöbl. La sciolina dei campioni
1935

Color lithograph on paper
Private Collection

ERNST DRYDEN

Four designs for a woman's ski suit

c. 1921–1933

Pencil and watercolor on paper
Hamburg, Museum für Kunst und Gewerbe Hamburg

Ernst Dryden was a prominent figure in the fashion and graphic design world of his time, distinguishing himself as a designer and artist. His biography testifies to a remarkable skill in working on the international stage. Active in various commercial sectors, he traveled constantly between major cities in search of emerging trends.

UNKNOWN AUTHOR
Model in a ski suit
1935

Silver salt print on card
Warsaw, Szukaj w Archiwach

ERIK HOLMÉN
Model in skiwear
1938

Silver salt print on card
Stockholm, Nordiska museet

The two photographs show models wearing ski suits similar to those designed by Ernst Dryden.

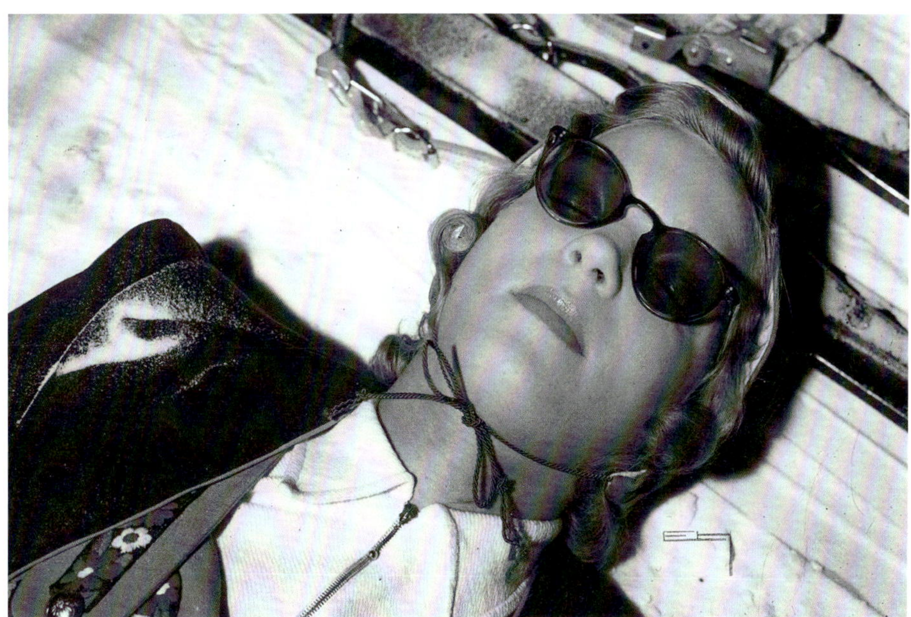

HENRY WECLAWOWICZ (WECLA)
Cover of Voici la mode
December 1935

Color lithograph on paper
Paris, Bibliothèque Nationale de France

aco, DIE SPORTMODE
Ski suit
c. 1930

Massa Lombarda, Archivi Mazzini

ASPEN [US]

L. FÉRRIER (?)
Winter sports, in Voici la mode
December 1935

Color lithograph on paper
Paris, Bibliothèque Nationale de France

VOICI *la* MODE *de* DÉCEMBRE 1935

SPORTS D'HIVER

Hardiesse des couleurs et netteté des lignes.

Costume de ski, en burnow bleu. La veste croisée est ornée de larges revers; les accessoires sont en laine bordeaux et blanche.

Veste en cuir avec fermeture éclair, pantalon en gabardine imperméable.

Les accessoires qui accompagnent ce costume ont été choisis en laine rouge, s'harmonisant parfaitement avec le ton vert; des passepoils soulignent les coutures de la veste et celles des poches au pantalon.

Ce manteau d'ocelot ou de panthère complétera votre garde-robe pour sports d'hiver; vous le voyez avec une jupe de gros lainage et une blouse tricotée, en laine jaune, écharpe et gants assortis à la jupe.

Costume en burella marron avec pantalon plus-four; les accessoires sont en tricot mandarine; la veste est fixée par une fermeture éclair.

Cette cape, en manyfil de Rodier, que vous doublerez de fourrure, sera très nouvelle sur votre costume de patinage.

20

Ce manteau en gabardine imperméable doublé de flanelle accompagnera votre costume de patinage, le col et les revers sont en phoque; jupe en lainage marron et blouse en lainage écossais bleu pastel et marron.

Les accessoires de ce costume sont en tricot rouge vif; la veste et le pantalon sont en gabardine imperméable bleu marine, des poches verticales sont prises dans les coutures de la veste, fixées par un bouton.

Cette jeune femme porte un gilet d'ocelot sur son costume de ski fait en burella amadou accompagné d'accessoires en tricot vert.

Un pantalon de drap marron, accompagné d'une veste en loden blanc boutonnée de cuir compose une tenue des plus élégante et pratique.

Un gilet en peau de mouton, avec poches piquées main complète ce costume de drap vert; au pantalon knicker, les poches en biais prolongent la couture.

21

MAISON LAPPARRA, PARIS
Femina Grisons Ski Cup
c.1935

Silver-plated brass and marble
Private Collection

Trophy created for the Femina Ski Cup, a prestigious international women's ski competition organized in the Grisons region since the 1920s. Promoted by the French magazine *Femina*, the competition was one of the main sporting and social events for the European elite, celebrating the emergence of women in competitive skiing and winter tourism.

CASSANDRE (ADOLPHE JEAN MARIE MOURON)
Sketch for the Dubonnet logo—Ice skater
c.1932

CASSANDRE (ADOLPHE JEAN MARIE MOURON)
Sketch for the Dubonnet logo—Skier
c.1932

Pencil on paper
Private Collection

CASSANDRE (ADOLPHE JEAN MARIE MOURON)
Advertising poster for the Dubonnet Cup
1939

Lithograph on paper
Private Collection

This advertising poster promotes the Coupe Dubonnet, a ski competition held in Chamonix on March 12, 1939. The name is that of the famous aperitif, with the slogan "Dubo, Dubon, Dubonnet" and the iconic logo created by graphic designer Cassandre in 1932. The race, which took place on the slopes of the glaciers at the foot of the Aiguille du Midi, was a downhill race organized jointly by the town of Chamonix, local tourist operators, and sports clubs.

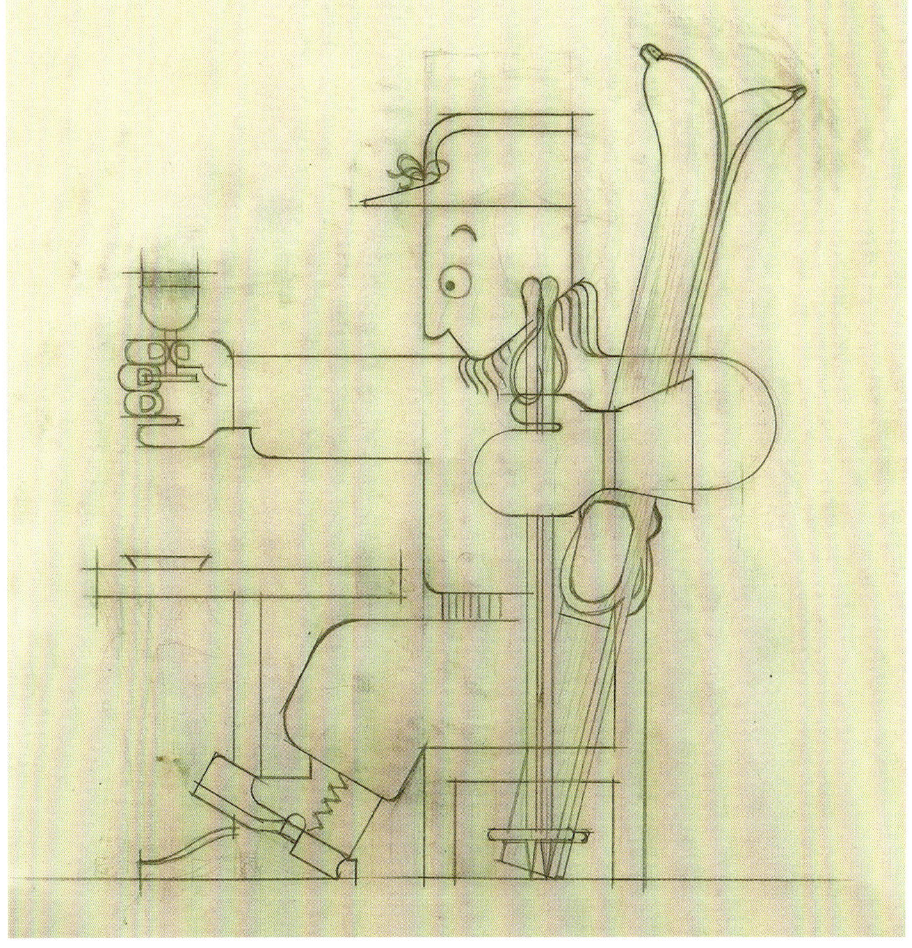

GIO PONTI x SOCIETÀ CERAMICA RICHARD-GINORI, DOCCIA
Six plates from the Sports series
c. 1930

Porcelain
Private Collection

GIO PONTI x SOCIETÀ CERAMICA RICHARD-GINORI, DOCCIA
Pair of cups from the Sports series—Skiing
1936

Porcelain
Rosignano Marittimo, Collezione Raffaello Pernici - Best Ceramics

ALEX WALTER DIGGELMANN
Passez vos vacances a Interlaken. Suisse
c. 1940

Chromolithograph on paper
Private Collection

GERHARD RIEBICKE
Waiters on skates serve drinks to guests on the ice rink of the Grand Hotel in St. Moritz
c. 1925

Black and white print
Private Collection

F.L. FRAUK (AFTER)
La Nuit du Ski
1931

Color lithograph on paper
Private Collection

RENÉ PROU (MODEL)
AUGUSTE BERLIN, AFTER SIMON LISSIM (DÉCOR)
x MANUFACTURE NATIONAL DE SÈVRES, PARIS
Les Skis
1937

Porcelain
Rosignano Marittimo, Collezione Raffaello Pernici – Best Ceramics

This large Sèvres vase displays a snowy mountain landscape over its entire exterior, with silhouettes of mountains in several shades of cool colours. A skier is shown whose figure gradually becomes more visible as the vase is rotated, appearing to reach the summit before beginning a descent.

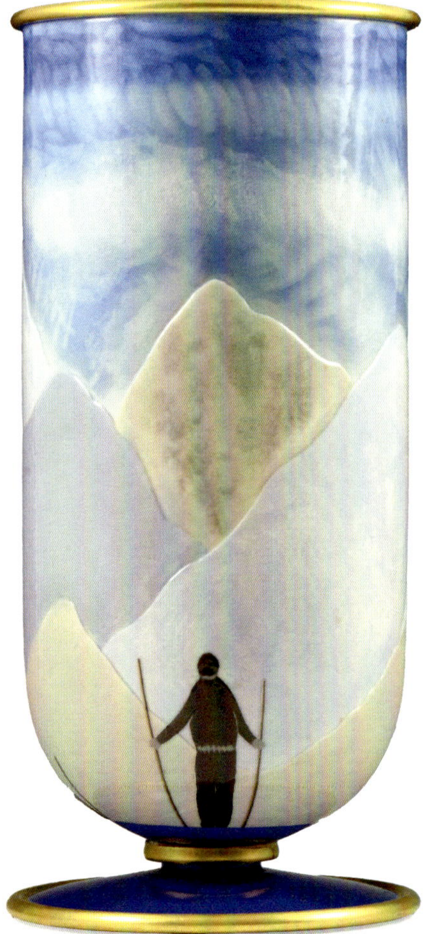

ROMEN WYLCAN E WLADYSLAW ROZANSKI
Zima w Polsce
1935

Color lithograph on card
Private Collection

ZIMA W POLSCE
POLSKA POLAND POLEN POLOGEN
M. RÓŻAŃSKI
R. WYŁCAN
PRINTED IN POLAND
NAKŁADEM MINISTERSTWA KOMUNIKACJI
ZAKŁ. GRAF. E. i Dr. K. KOZIAŃSKICH, WARSZAWA.

EDWARD HALD AND ERNST ÅBERG

Bandy players

1936

Engraved glass and wood
Stockholm, Nordiska museet

The trophy made for the 1936 Berlin Olympics depicts the game of bandy, a team sport traditionally played in northern Europe (Russia, Sweden, Norway, and Finland) and similar to ice hockey. It is played by two teams of eleven players on a frozen field the size of a football pitch. The aim of the game is to score a point by hitting a small hard ball into the opponent's goal using a bandy stick.

ERNST LUDWIG KIRCHNER

Hockey players

1934

Oil on canvas
Private Collection

Ernst Ludwig Kirchner painted this work in 1934. It is a clear example of his deep interest in the expressive power of lines and the intensity of colors. The painting was probably executed during the artist's stay in Switzerland, where winter sports played an important role.

PIERO PORTALUPPI

La stella di neve—Corsa d'auto e gara di sci

1934

Black marble, silver metal, and cut crystal
Private Collection, courtesy Il Ponte Casa d'Aste

In Piero Portaluppi's characteristic style, the trophy is a schematic miniature of the road through the Formazza valley, the hotel, and the Toce waterfall. The hotel was restored and extended by the Milanese architect between 1925 and 1929. The project was part of an industrial and tourist development plan led by Piero Portaluppi with the Girola company and the industrialist Ettore Conti. The plan also included the construction of the Wagristoratore restaurant (1929–1930, now demolished) at Passo San Giacomo, accessible by car and created in two railway carriages.

HENRI DORMOY
Antar-Gel
c.1920

Color lithograph on paper
Private Collection

ALF DANNING
Kun näkyväisyys on huono
c. 1935

Color lithograph on paper
Private Collection

Advertising poster for a Finnish insurance company promoting road safety in poor visibility conditions. The message urges drivers not to be distracted by openings in the forest when visibility is reduced.

ANONYMOUS
La 1500 invita al Sestriere
1935

Color lithograph on paper
Private Collection

ANONYMOUS
Dans une Renault...
1936

Color lithograph on paper
Private Collection

JAPANESE MANUFACTURE

Japan at the Winter Olympics

c. 1930

Printed silk and cotton
Melbourne, National Gallery of Victoria

The *omoshirogara* (funny drawings) depicted fashions, popular events, and technological advances of the time and were printed on the inner linings of *haori* (short jackets) and *nagajuban* (long undergarments worn under kimonos). Also present were news items and popular sports, such as Japan's success at the 1928 Winter Olympics.

TEODORO SEBELIN

Pair of skiers

1930–1938

Ceramic
Rosignano Marittimo, Collezione Raffaello Pernici - Best Ceramics

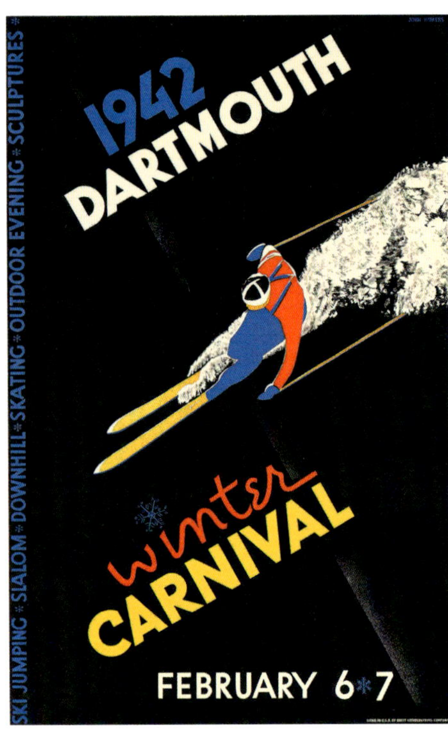

JOHN R. BOWERS
Dartmouth. Winter Carnival
1942

Color lithograph on paper
Private Collection

JAPANESE ARTIST
Commemoration of the eighth edition of the Japanese National Student Ski Competition
1935

Color lithograph on card
Boston, Museum of Fine Arts, Collezione Leonard A. Lauder

CZESLAW WIELHORSKI
FIS. Ski Championships of the World
1939

Color lithograph on paper
Private Collection

GASTON GORDE
Downhill - Skier
1934

Color lithograph on paper
Private Collection

PIERRE KRAMER
Zermatt—26th Skirennen
1931

Color lithograph on paper
Private Collection

ATELIER KIRNIG
Austria
1937

Color lithograph on paper
Private Collection

EMILIO MONTI
Downhill Skier
1941

Aluminum and white marble
Private Collection, courtesy Il Ponte Casa d'Aste

PAOLO FEDERICO GARRETTO
Cover of Adam magazine
November 15, 1937

Color lithograph on paper
Private Collection

RAYMOND DE LAVERERIE
Cover of Adam magazine
November 15, 1938

Color lithograph on paper
Private Collection

PAOLO FEDERICO GARRETTO
Cover of Adam magazine
January 15, 1936

Color lithograph on paper
Private Collection

PAOLO FEDERICO GARRETTO
Cover of Adam magazine
January 15, 1937

Color lithograph on paper
Private Collection

RAYMOND DE LAVERERIE
Cover of Adam magazine
November 1, 1945

Color lithograph on paper
Private Collection

PAOLO FEDERICO GARRETTO
Cover of Adam magazine
January 15, 1938

Color lithograph on paper
Private Collection

MATADOR
Embroidered padded ski jacket
c. 1940

Massa Lombarda, Archivi Mazzini

ZEBRA MODELL
Ski suit: jacket with hood and trousers
c. 1940

Massa Lombarda, Archivi Mazzini

BÜELENHORN [CH] 

ROSSIGNOL
Olympic 41
(detail and overall view)
1941

ROSSIGNOL
Allais
1960

ROSSIGNOL
Strato
1965

Photo Archivio Rossignol

ABEL ROSSIGNOL
Patents
1942–1954

UNKNOWN PHOTOGRAPHER
Skier
c. 1940

Black and white print
Photo Archivio Rossignol

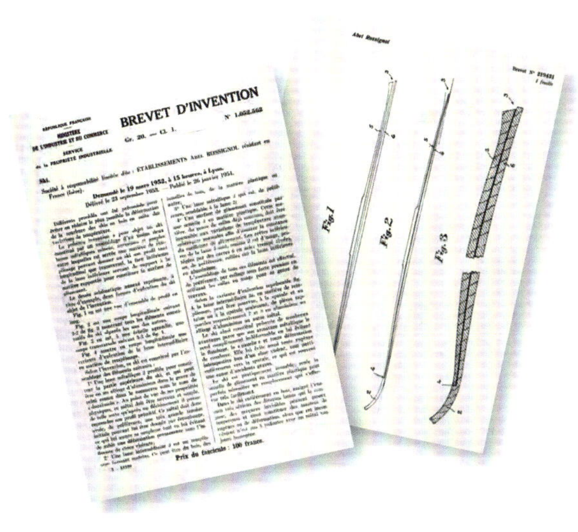
BREVET D'INVENTION

Fig.1

Fig.2

Fig.3

In 1939, for the first time, Abel Rossignol applied the lamination of wood to the manufacture of skis, a technological innovation that solved problems with performance and strength. This marked the beginning of a series of research projects that led to a number of patents, such as the 1939 patent for laminated skis made from a single type of wood and the 1942 patent (219431) for skis made from different types of wood laminated together, which would lead to the creation of the Olympic 41—the first modern ski that abandoned solid wood in favor of a layered structure of glued wooden strips made up of base, core, and upper section. These skis, which guaranteed greater solidity and better performance on snow, were produced continuously until 1965.

UNKNOWN MANUFACTURE
High-altitude goggles
Mid-twentieth century

Leather, glass, and metal
Montebelluna, Archivio Prodotti Fondazione Sportsystem

UNKNOWN MANUFACTURE
High-altitude goggles
Mid-twentieth century

Leather, plastic resin (probably CR-39), elastic tape, and metal
Montebelluna, Archivio Prodotti Fondazione Sportsystem

UNKNOWN MANUFACTURE
High altitude goggles
Mid-twentieth century

Fabric, plastic resin (probably CR-39), elastic tape, and metal
Montebelluna, Archivio Prodotti Fondazione Sportsystem

These three models of goggles were used by some members of the Italian expedition to K2 in 1954. Given the variety, it can be assumed that each participant was able to choose one or more models according to their personal requirements.

FOTO GIACOTTO
Advertisement for Persol glasses, in Bellezza
July 1944

Print on paper
Private Collection

Marina Berti, star alongside Amedeo Nazzari in Renato Castellani's film *La donna della montagna* (1943), was chosen by Persol to advertise its sunglasses.

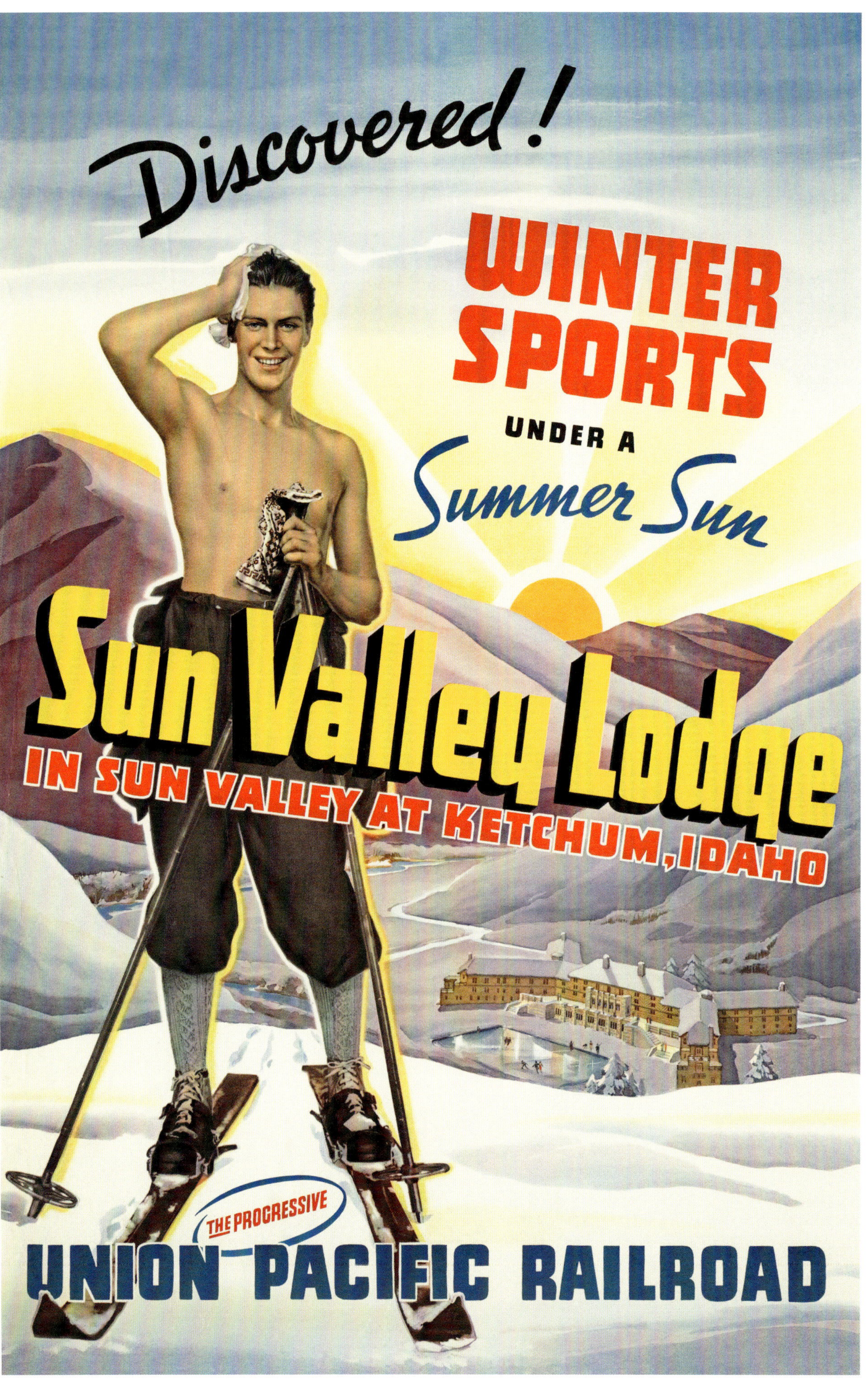

UNKNOWN ARTIST
Sun Valley Lodge. Union Pacific Railroad
c. 1940

Color lithograph on paper
Boston, Public Library

The poster advertises the Sun Valley Lodge in Idaho, a famous ski resort offering winter sports under the summer sun. The composition captures the energy of the mountains and their accessibility via the Union Pacific rail service. A suggestive depiction of a shirtless man with a charming, relaxed expression invites the viewer to imagine a dynamic, sensual holiday where sports and relaxation come together under the sun.

PIERRE (LAURENT) BRENOT
Marie des neiges
1952

PIERRE (LAURENT) BRENOT
A glance back
1950

PIERRE (LAURENT) BRENOT
Downhill follie
1950

Color lithograph on paper
Private Collection

Cover for Modern Screen
February 1948

Color lithograph on paper
Private Collection

The photograph shows actress Shirley Temple wearing the typical and now iconic red sweater that characterizes all the "glam" skiers depicted in Tamara de Lempicka's painting and the sweater by Jean Patou.

Cover for Ebony
February 1949

Color lithograph on paper
New York, Public Library

Founded by the Black publisher John Harold Johnson, *Ebony* began publication in the autumn of 1945. Following in the footsteps of the more popular and better-selling *Life*, *Ebony* has always focused on showcasing the success of people of African American origin, presenting them in a positive light. Thanks to this publishing initiative, for the first time numerous companies and industries across the country began to feature Black models and actors in their advertisements in Johnson's magazine.

Cover for The Australian Women Weekly
June 12, 1948

Color lithograph on paper
Private Collection

OZZIE SWEET
Cover for Modern Photography
January 1953

Color lithograph on paper
Private Collection

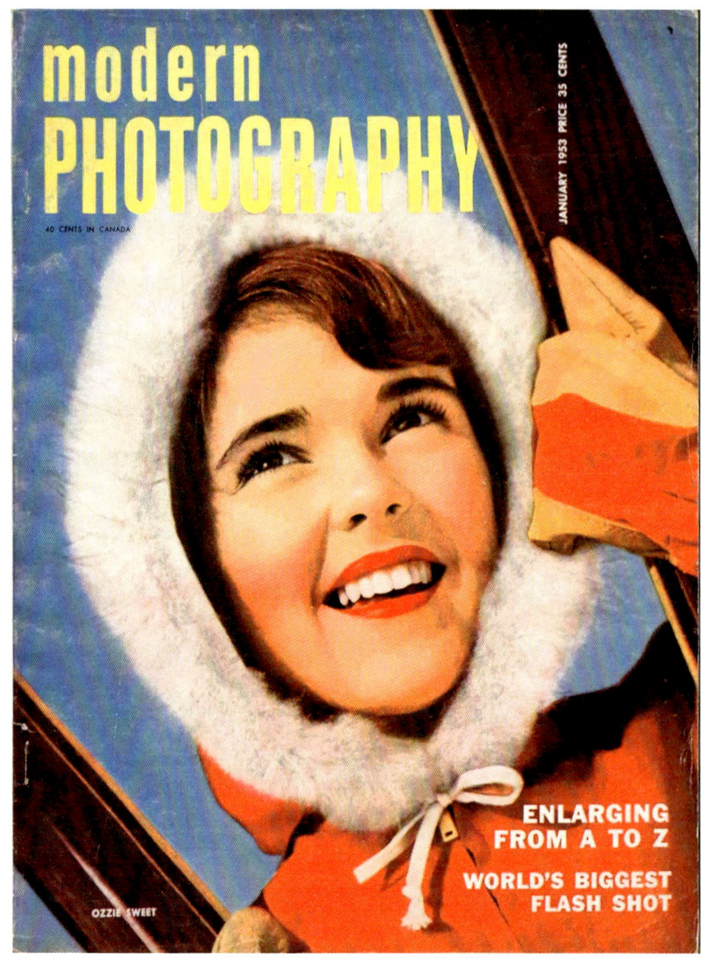

EBONY
In This Issue
HOW I WAS CHEATED
OUT OF $500,000
By Beau Jack
SKIING: NEW FAVORITE
AS NEGRO WINTER SPORT
FEBRUARY 1949 30c

IT'S SNOWING!

BLOMER & SCHÜLER
Woman Skier
1940-1950

Lithographed sheet metal
Private Collection

JAPANESE MANUFACTURE
Bear on skis
1950-1960

Lithographed sheet metal
Private Collection

BLOMER & SCHÜLER
Woman Skier
1940-1950

Lithographed sheet metal
Private Collection

SHANGHAI KANG YUAN TOY FACTORY
Chinese child on skis
c. 1960

Lithographed sheet metal
Private Collection

JAPANESE MANUFACTURE
Skier
1950-1960

Lithographed sheet metal
Private Collection

LEHMANN
"Skirolf–EPL 781" skier
1930-1941

Lithographed sheet metal
Private Collection

LA DOLOMITE
Advertisement
c. 1961

Black and white print
Courtesy Dolomite

LA DOLOMITE
Lino Lacedelli on K2
1954

Black and white print
Courtesy Dolomite

Founded in 1897 by Giuseppe Garbuio in Montebelluna as Fabbrica Scarpe Montello, La Dolomite is one of the leading names in the history of mountaineering and Italian design. On July 31, 1954, at 6 p.m., Achille Compagnoni and Lino Lacedelli reached the summit of K2 for the first time wearing handmade La Dolomite mountain boots. La Dolomite has supplied other memorable expeditions: in 1960, the Dhaulagiri, the last unclimbed eight-thousander; in 1976, the Fitz Roy, reached by the Ragni di Lecco climbing team. Apart from mountaineering, La Dolomite also made its mark in the field of design and was the first sports brand to receive the Compasso d'Oro design award in 1957, a prize it won again in 1967. During this expedition, padded goose down suits fastened with elastic bands were used for the first time to ensure maximum thermal insulation.

Al servizio degli Alpinisti e delle Guide dal 1897; ha raccolto negli ultimi anni una messe imponente di Vittorie Alpine.

la Dolomite

è stata adottata dalle seguenti

Spedizioni Extra - Europee:

Spedizione Italiana 1954 al Karakorum - K 2
Spedizione De Agostini 1955 alla Terra del Fuoco
Spedizione Triestina 1955 alla Catena del Tauro
Spedizione Milanese 1957 ai Monti del Centro Africa
Spedizione Triestina 1957 all'Elburz
Spedizione Italiana 1957-58 alle Ande Patagoniche
Kordilleren Kundfahrt 1957 des Osterreichischen Alpenvereins
Spedizione Bonatti - Mauri 1958 al Cerro Torre
Spedizione Milanese 1958 alle Ande Peruviane
Spedizione Torinese 1958 alle Ande Peruviane
Spedizione Comasca 1958 alle Ande Peruviane
Spedizione Ghiglione - Pirovano 1958 in Columbia
Spedizione Italiana 1958 al Karakorum - Gasherbrum IV
British Caucasus Expedition 1958
Spedizione G. M. 1959 al Karakorum
Spedizione Bergamasca 1960 alle Ande Peruviane
Schweizerische Himalaya Expedition 1960 Dhaulagiri
Spedizione G. M. 1960 al 66° Parallelo - Groenlandia Occidentale
Spediz. Torinese 1961 alle Ande - Cordillera Bianca
Expedicion Espagnola 1961 a los Andes del Perù
Norwegian Himalayan Expedition 1961 - Chitral
Spedizione Lecchese 1961 in Alaska - Monte Mac Kinley

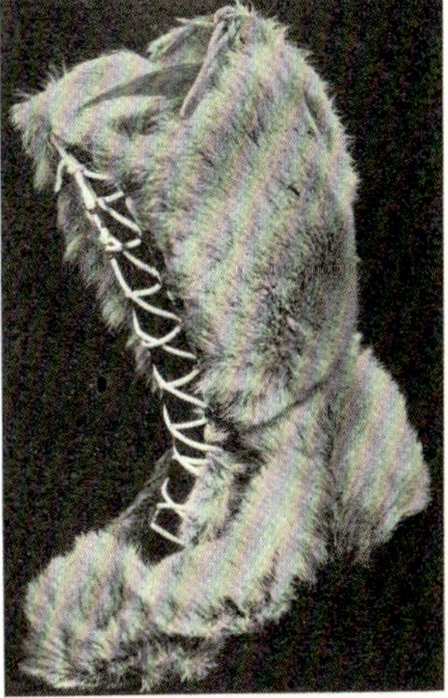

Art. 10 - STIVALE PER ALTITUDINE

Stivale in Renna fornito alla Spedizione Italiana al K 2 - Karakorum 1954.

Bottes en Renne employées par l'Expedition Italienne au K 2 Karakorum 1954.

Reindeer boots supplied to the Italian Expedition to K 2 (Godwin Austen) Karakoram 1954.

Art. 11 - STIVALETTO POLARE

LA DOLOMITE
High altitude boot
1954

Reindeer leather and fur, wool felt, leather, vulcanized rubber, small metal parts
Montebelluna, Archivio Prodotti Fondazione Sportsystem

With this La Dolomite-produced model, Lino Lacedelli and Achille Compagnoni reached the summit of K2 for the first time in July 1954. The success of the expedition led by professor Ardito Desio was such that K2 has since been known as "the mountain of the Italians." This particular model is the one worn by Lino Lacedelli.

LA DOLOMITE
High altitude ankle boot
1954

Reindeer leather and fur, wool felt, leather, vulcanized rubber, small metal parts
Montebelluna, Archivio Prodotti Fondazione Sportsystem

These boots, made of reindeer leather, were part of the equipment developed by La Dolomite for the 1954 expedition to K2. The model shown in the image was worn by Achille Compagnoni. The same model was later marketed as "luxury snow boots" and featured in the company's catalogue over the following decade.

FRANCO GRIGNANI
Cover of Bellezza d'Italia, *no. 6*
1953

Lithograph on paper
Private Collection

FRANCO GRIGNANI
Cover of Bellezza d'Italia, *no. 2*
1956

Lithograph on paper
Private Collection

FRANCO GRIGNANI
Cover of Bellezza d'Italia, *no. 1*
1950

Lithograph on paper
Private Collection

FRANCO GRIGNANI
Dompé advertisement in Bellezza d'Italia, *no. 2*
1956

Lithograph on paper
Private Collection

← Launched in 1947 by Franco Dompé, *Bellezza d'Italia* was a magazine for doctors that combined articles on travel, art, fashion, and sport with high-impact advertisements for Dompé pharmaceutical products. Franco Grignani, one of the most visionary designers of the time, was chosen as art director to create a magazine that would celebrate the beauty of Italian cities and promoted the company's values with an innovative and refined design. He also established collaborations with some of the greatest Italian authors and journalists of the time, such as Dino Buzzati, Indro Montanelli, and Camilla Cederna. The elegant design of the magazine and the prominent personalities involved in the project soon bore fruit. In 1955, Franco Grignani decided to redesign the layout of *Bellezza d'Italia*, as several imitations began to appear. From that year onwards, the magazine was printed in landscape format instead of portrait. Beginning in 1956, the magazine also set out for markets outside Italy with translations into English, German, and Spanish. The last issue, of over seventy published, came out in 1962.

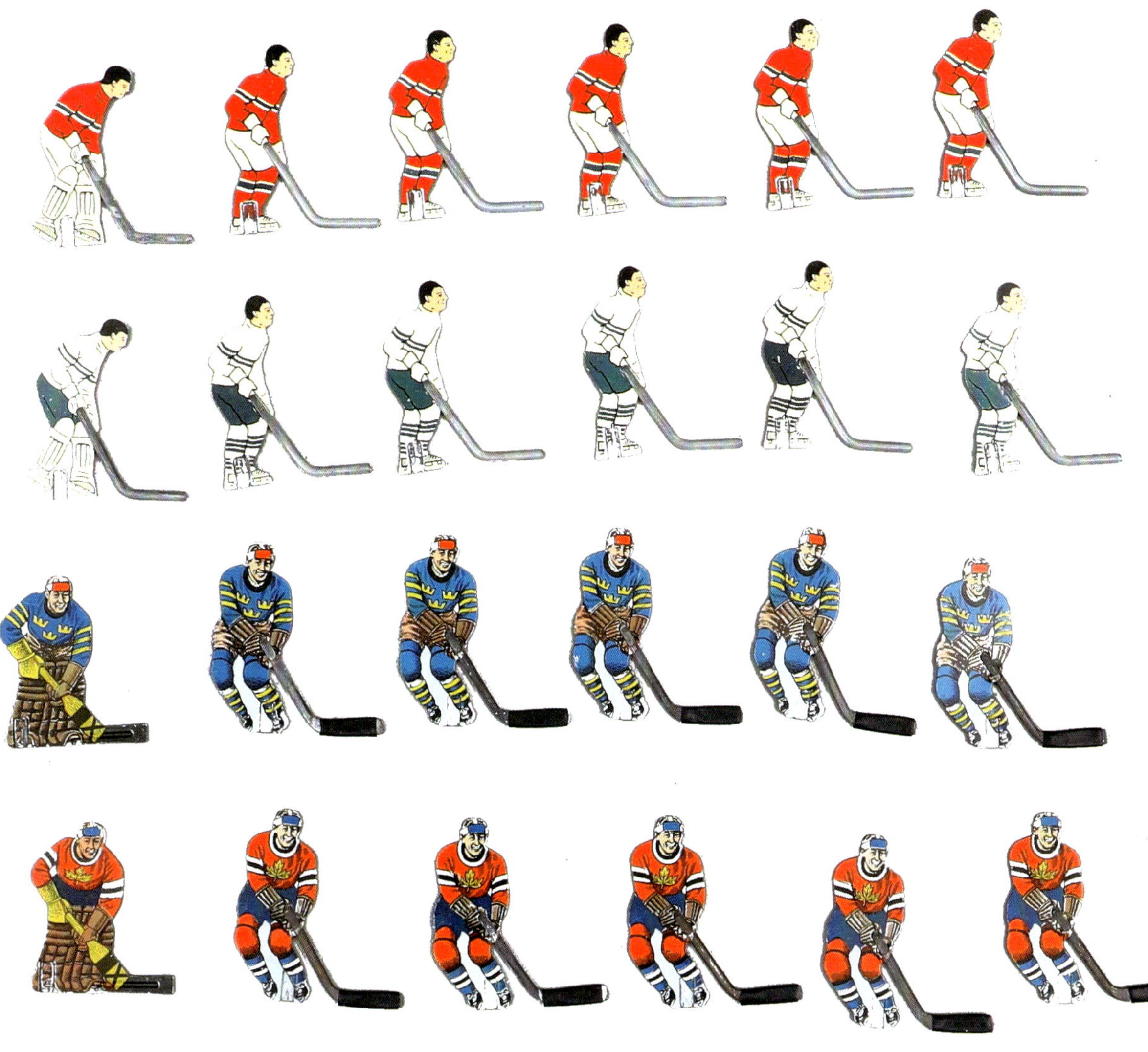

ARISTOSPEL

Ice hockey game and players—Puck

1950–1960

Plastic, metal, and lithograph on paper
Private Collection

The Puck board game, produced in the 1950s, was the first of its kind to simulate an ice hockey game. Created by Aristospel, a Swedish company founded in 1936, the game became iconic in its genre, giving rise to a new form of entertainment for sports fans.

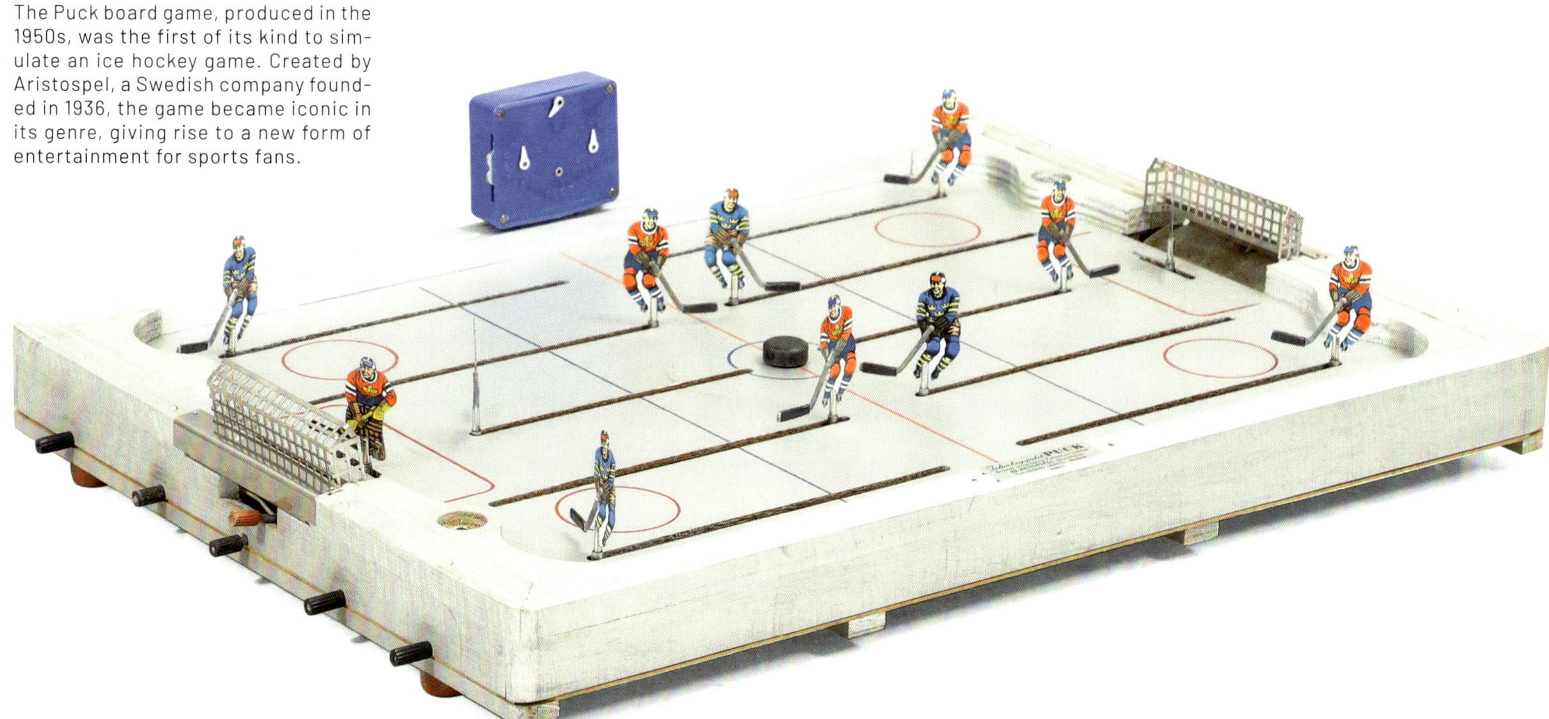

IO CREDEVO CHE LA MIA NEVE FOSSE **BIANCA**!
GIÀ, MA LA MIA E' **LEVATA** CON **UOMO**!
BRRR
CHE FENOMENO... DODICI MINUTI... CI HAI MESSO SOLO LA **METÀ**!
PER LA GARA IN CORSO CI SERVONO SOLO BOB A **QUATTRO**!
HO IMPARATO A SCIARE L'ESTATE SCORSA A VIAREGGIO!
OGGI STO SCIANDO CON NEVE PESANTE!
L'ANULARE, INVECE, ME LO SON ROTTO SCIANDO...
TU IL FREDDO LO SENTI DI PIÙ ALLA TESTA?
VERAMENTE IO PREFERIREI SCALDARMI CON UN COGNACCHINO!
OGGI HO UN **TREMENDO** RAFFREDDORE.
A METÀ PERCORSO SONO STATO INVESTITO DA UNA VALANGA..
PISTA.... **PISTAA... PISTAAA!!!**
PERO' QUESTI SCIATORI CONGELATI SON FACILI DA TRASPORTARE...
E IO INVECE SON CADUTO **QUATTRO** VOLTE!
OGGI SI AFFONDA FACILMENTE NELLA NEVE!
MA QUESTO NON È IL MAGLIONE DI TUO FRATELLO?

JACOVITTI

BRRR!

1958

Ink on paper
Private Collection

Benito Jacovitti, born in Termoli, Molise, is acknowledged as one of the greatest Italian cartoonists of the twntieth century, with a vast output characterized by a rich personal rich style with surreal details. He earned his place in the history of Italian comics above all thanks to the caricature-like appearance of his characters. The characteristic anatomical shape of the small figures that he brought to life on paper, their sometimes joyful sometimes grotesque expressions, his cold cuts and sliced meats, snakes and snails with all kinds of expressions, as well as many other objects scattered in the most unexpected places, made him popular with the general public.

EUGENE M. CORDIER

Für Winterreisen Deutsche Bundesbahn

1952

Color lithograph on paper
Private Collection

In the 1950s, the German railways promoted Germany as a destination for winter sports, using humor to attract tourists. The poster depicts a woman in skiwear, a symbol of modernity and speed, with the Fliegender train (the fastest and most elegant of its kind) in the background, reinforcing the concept of the convenience of travelling to ski resorts by train.

HANS JEGERLEHNER

Zum Wintersport mit der Eisenbahn

1950

Color lithograph on paper
Private Collection

HUGO WETLI

CFF—Départ pour le soleil d'hiver

1958

Color lithograph on paper
Private Collection

CARLO DRADI

neve al Campo dei fiori—Ferrovie Nord Milano

1947-1960

Color lithograph on paper
Private Collection

WALTER HARNISCH

ÖBB-Auch-im-Winter...

1955

Color lithograph on paper
Private Collection

NIERHAUS + ESTENFELDER
Deutsche Bundesbahn
1959

Color lithograph on paper
Private Collection

MARTIN PEIKERT
St. Moritz—Piz Nair
c.1948

Color lithograph on paper
Private Collection

UNKNOWN ARTIST
Japan Ski Skating Sunshine
1950

Color lithograph on paper
Private Collection

The poster advertises the train journey to Nikko, a famous Japanese tourist destination, with an illustration of skaters and skiers in action. The advertisement highlights the importance of trains in bringing tourists to ski resorts and mountain landscapes, making winter destinations more accessible to everyone.

スキースケートは
日光へ
東武電車
日光町

HANS FALK
Sport au Soleil en Suisse
c. 1960-1965

Color lithograph on paper
Private Collection

PAOLO MARIONI
Woman skier
c. 1960

Majolica
Rosignano Marittimo, Collezione Raffaello Pernici – Best Ceramics

RICHARD JOSEPH NEUTRA
Sunshine
1957

Pastel on paper
Los Angeles, UCLA, Library Special Collections, Charles E. Young Research Library

RICHARD JOSEPH NEUTRA
Ski Banff, Canada
1956

Pastel on paper
Los Angeles, UCLA, Library Special Collections, Charles E. Young Research Library

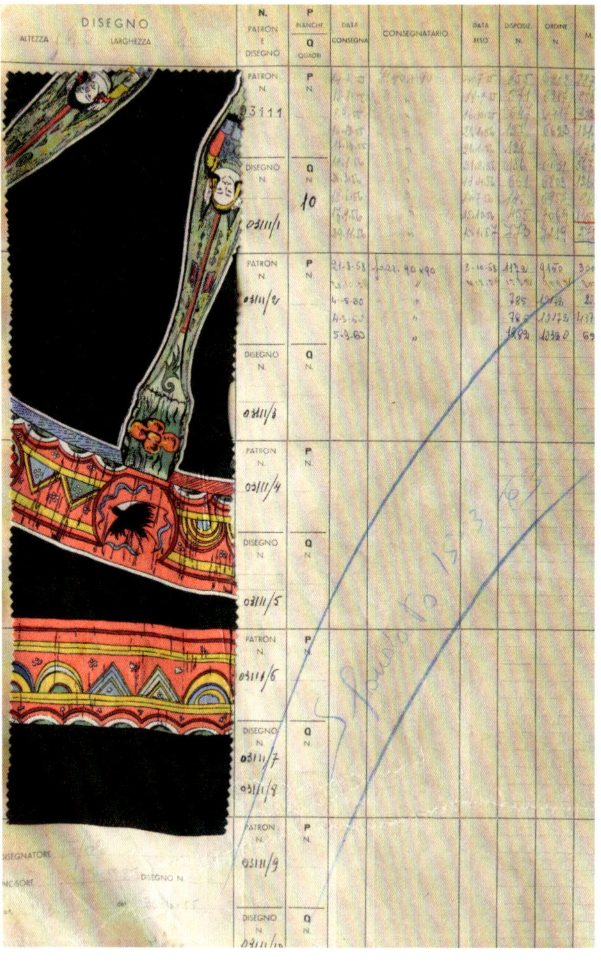

TONI FRISSELL
Letha Gilbert in Zermatt
1956

Color print
Washington D.C., Library of Congress

EMILIO PUCCI
Ruota siciliana *with product description*
1955

Printed silk twill fabric
Como, Fondazione Antonio Ratti

TONI FRISSELL
Letha Gilbert and Toni Frissell in Zermatt
1956

Color print
Washington D.C., Library of Congress

EMILIO PUCCI
Mosaico
1955

Tempera on parchment paper
Como, Fondazione Antonio Ratti

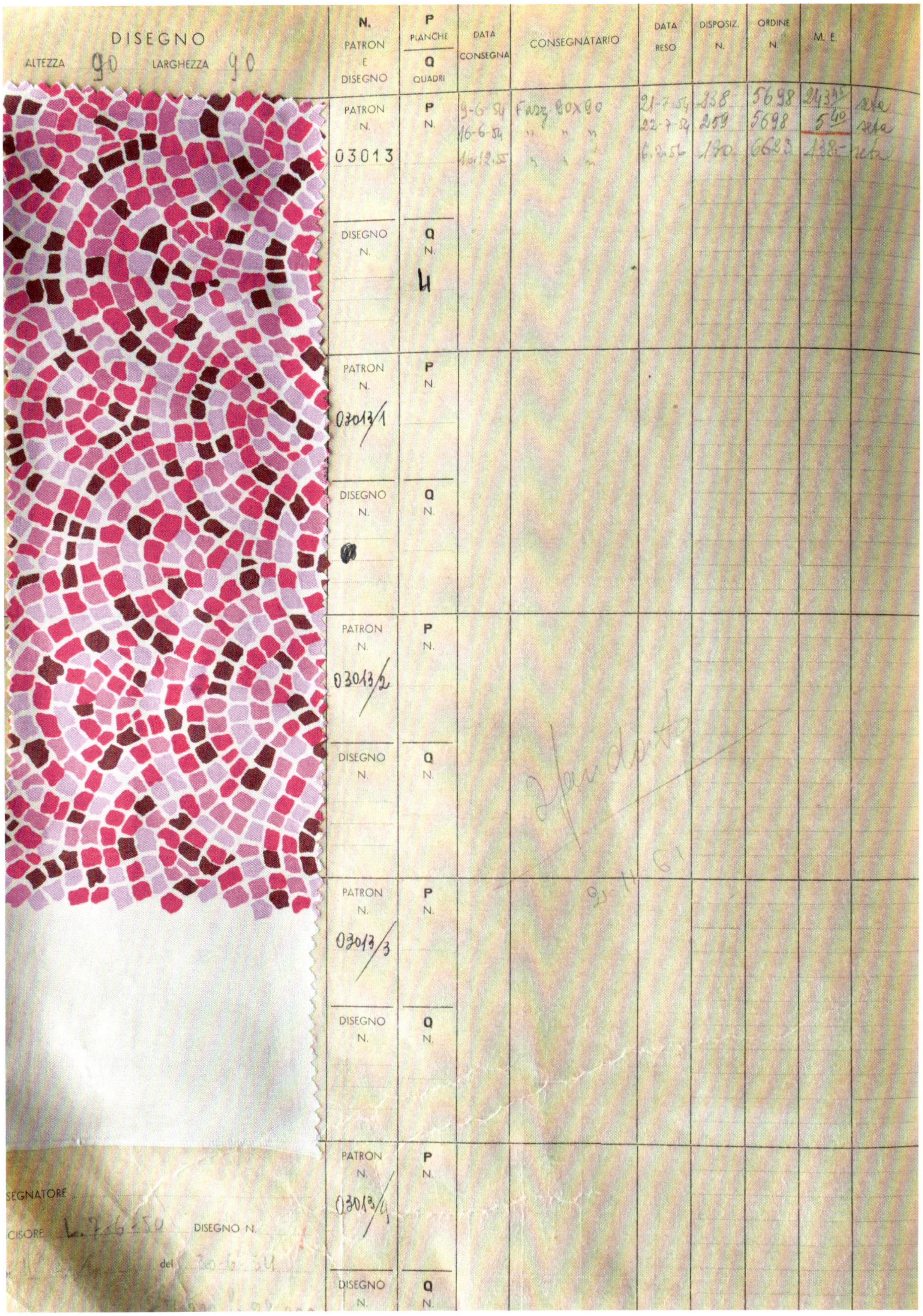

EMILIO PUCCI
Mosaico *with product description*
1954

Printed silk twill fabric
Como, Fondazione Antonio Ratti

Emilio Pucci was launched into the world of sportswear in 1947 in St. Moritz, where the marquis lent one of his own ski suits to a woman skier who didn't have one. The elegant and functional garment caught the attention of *Harper's Bazaar* photographer Toni Frissell, who encouraged him to develop a line for mass production. This led to a collaboration with the Ravasi weaving mill in Como, which was pivotal in translating the idea of refined and modern sportswear into fabric. Between 1951 and 1952, the first mountain-themed printed fabrics were produced, inspired by places such as Zermatt and Sestriere. The designs, produced by Giuseppe Ravasi, were remarkable for their subtle lines and quintessential style, reflecting Pucci's passion for the Alpine environment and the ski resorts frequented by the postwar jet set. These motifs anticipated the recognizable aesthetics of his subsequent collections, which alternated references to Sicilian culture, such as Carretto and mosaic prints, with Alpine subjects, applied to skiwear and après-ski boots. These garments were designed not only for sporting activities but also for the growing social après-ski ritual.

The numbers are estimated based on an analysis of resort lists provided by various mountain community websites and specialised travel and winter sports websites, with data updated as of July 15, 2025.

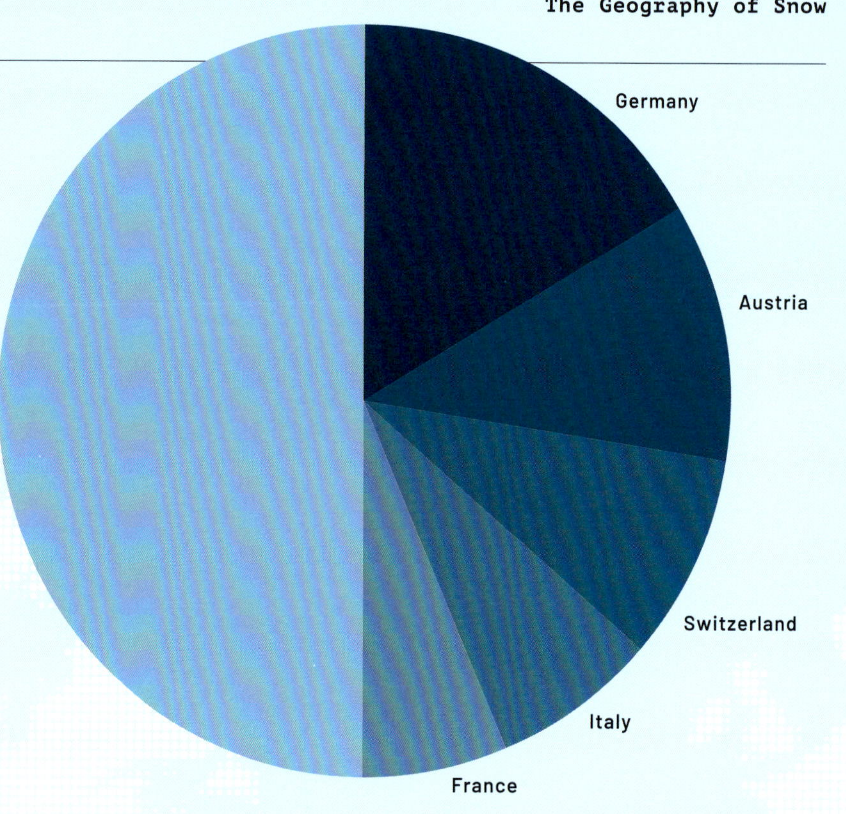

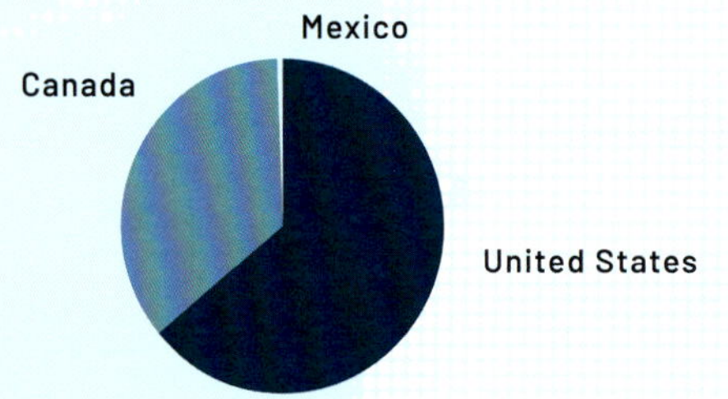

NORTH AND CENTRAL AMERICA

828 resorts

AFRICA

12 resorts

Others
Chile
Argentina

SOUTH AMERICA

44 resorts

EUROPE

3950 resorts

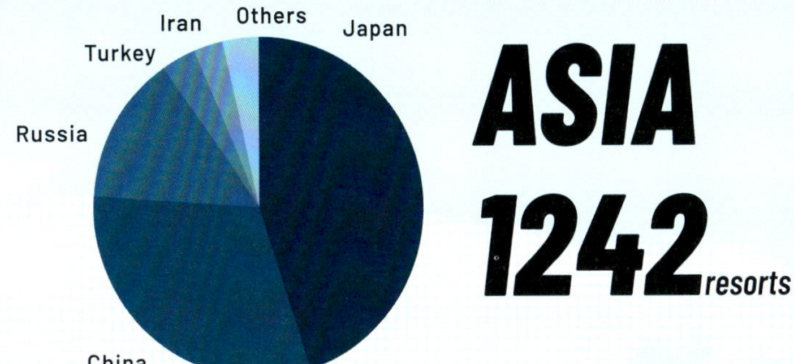

ASIA

1242 resorts

OCEANIA

51 resorts

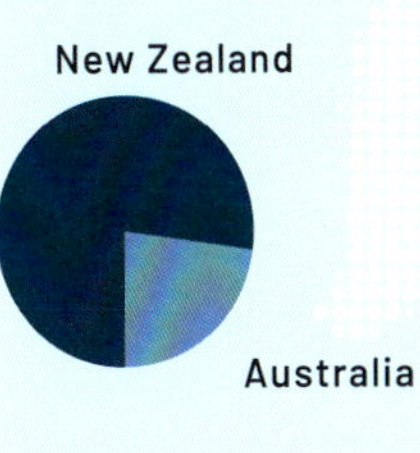

OTTO GLASER
Davos
1955

Color lithograph on paper
Private Collection

UNKNOWN ARTIST
La Province de Québec
c. 1940

Color lithograph on paper
Private Collection

MARTIN PEIKERT
Les Diablerets, chemin de fer Aigle-Sépey-Diablerets
1948

Color lithograph on paper
Private Collection

AMSTUTZ & HERDEG
Gstaad
1939

Color lithograph on paper
Private Collection

FRANCO BARBERIS
Klosters
c. 1950

Color lithograph on paper
Private Collection

MARIO PUPPO
Santo Stefano d'Aveto
c.1955

Color lithograph on paper
Private Collection

UNKNOWN ARTIST
Cortina d'Ampezzo
1920

Color lithograph on paper
Private Collection

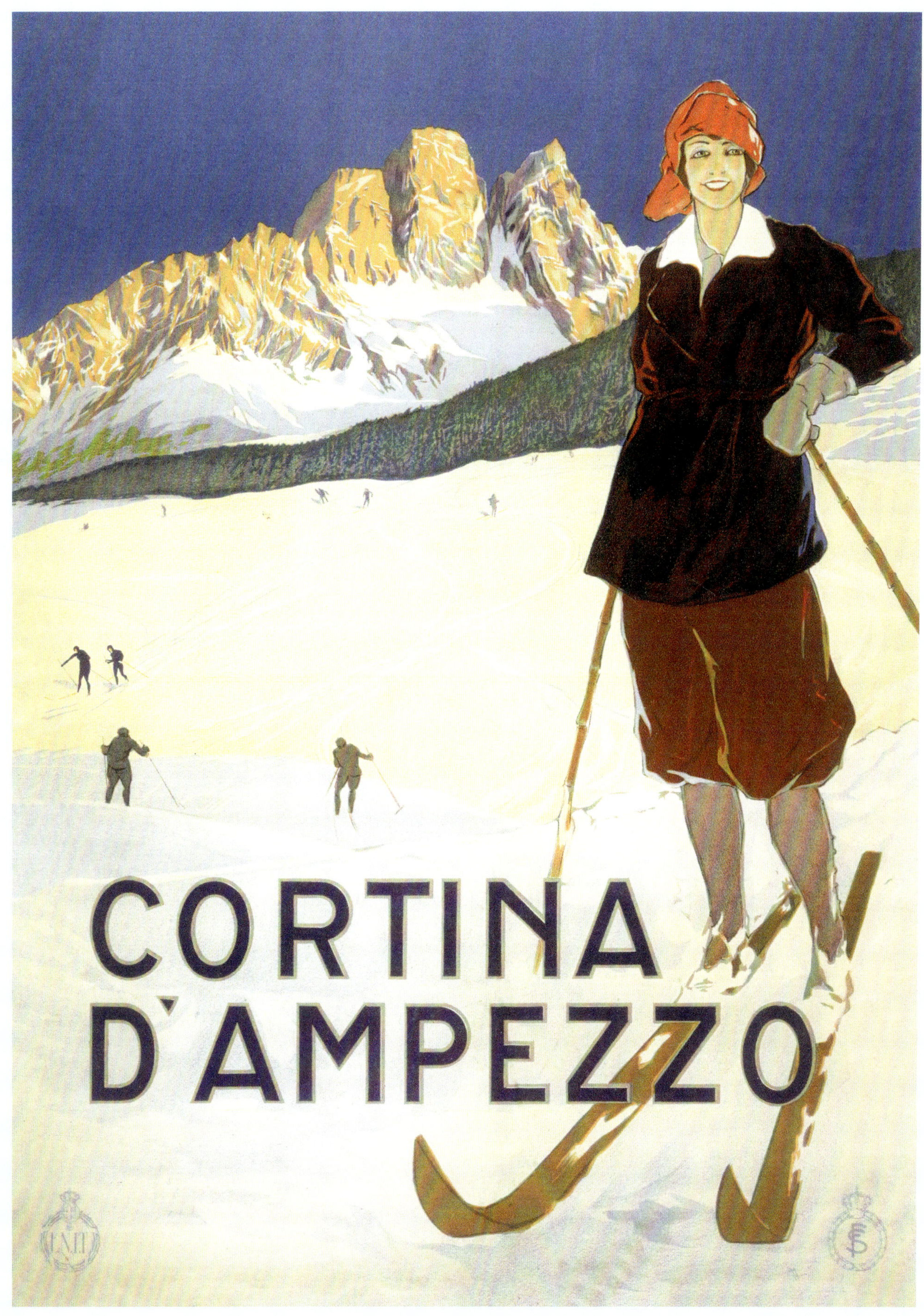

VOJTECH KUBASTA
Jasna Nízke Tatry
1951

Color lithograph on paper
Private Collection

ERIC DE COULON
Sports d'Hiver Alpes & Jura
1932

Color lithograph on paper
Private Collection

CORRADO MANCIOLI
10° Trofeo dell'Etna
1958

Color lithograph on paper
Private Collection

ERICH HERMÈS
Les Pléiades
c. 1929

Color lithograph on paper
Private Collection

MARIO PUPPO
Valle d'Aosta
1954

Color lithograph on paper
Private Collection

JANEZ TRPIN
Winter In Yugoslavia
1936

Color lithograph on paper
Private Collection

MARTIN PEIKERT
Wallis
1942

Color lithograph on paper
Private Collection

INGER SKJENSVOLD SØRENSEN
Norway, a Fistful of Fun
1956

Color lithograph on paper
Private Collection

HERBERT LEUPIN
Davos
1961

Color lithograph on paper
Private Collection

JEAN & LUCIEN GONGORO
Toujours le plus malin...
il a choisi le Valais Suisse
1951

Color lithograph on paper
Private Collection

UNKNOWN ARTIST
Dad, Mum, Me, a sporty family!
1977

Color lithograph on paper
Private Collection

HANS SCHILTER
Stoos, Schweiz, Suisse, Switzerland
1957

Color lithograph on paper
Private Collection

OTTO MALISCHKE
Arosa Ziel
1943

Color lithograph on paper
Private Collection

VILALLONGA
Supermolina
1954

Color lithograph on paper
Private Collection

R.A. JOHNSON
Sunny Alberta Winter Wonderland in the Canadian Rockies
1952

Color lithograph on paper
Private Collection

WILLIAM BORDIGONI
Champéry-PWoolchaux, Valais–Suisse
1947

Color lithograph on paper
Private Collection

UNKNOWN ARTIST
Säntis auch in Winter
c. 1960

Color lithograph on paper
Private Collection

UNKNOWN ARTIST
A Skier's Paradise Sun Valley Idaho
c. 1950

Color lithograph on paper
Private Collection

ADALBERTO CAMPAGNOLI
Torino Capitale delle Alpi
c. 1952

Color lithograph on paper
Private Collection

UNKNOWN ARTIST
Bardonecchia. Sole–Neve–Gioia di vivere
1939

Color lithograph on paper
Private Collection

WILLY TRAPP
Adelboden
c. 1930

Color lithograph on paper
Private Collection

J. HARPER
Kosciusko: for your holiday
c. 1936

Color lithograph on paper
Private Collection

G. PERÉS
Nuria
c. 1950

Color lithograph on paper
Private Collection

GEORGES AROU
Sports d'hiver
c. 1931

Color lithograph on paper
Private Collection

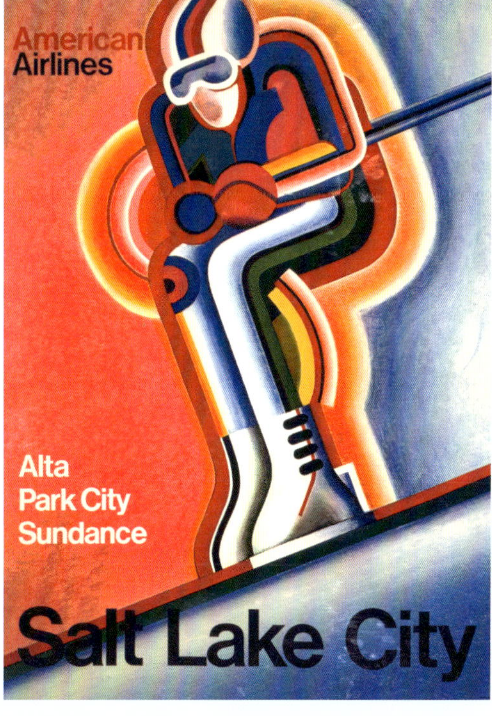

UNKNOWN ARTIST
Tsurugi Shishiku Highland
c. 1960

Color lithograph on paper
Private Collection

PAUL DEGEN
Alta Park City Sundance—Salt Lake City
1969

Color lithograph on paper
Private Collection

ITALO SPORT
Models presented at the first San Remo Fashion Festival Elasticated gabardine ski suits with shirt collars in the men's version
1952

Black and white photograph
Milan, Archivio Italo Sport

ITALO SPORT
Two ski suits photographed in the Milan store
c. 1958–1960

Colour photographs
Milan, Archivio Italo Sport

ITALO SPORT
Embroidered evening suit in stretch gabardine
c. 1959

Black and white photograph
Milan, Archivio Italo Sport

GIANPAOLA TAFFA x ITALO SPORT
Sketch for an embroidered evening suit in stretch gabardine
c. 1959

Ink on card
Milan, Archivio Italo Sport

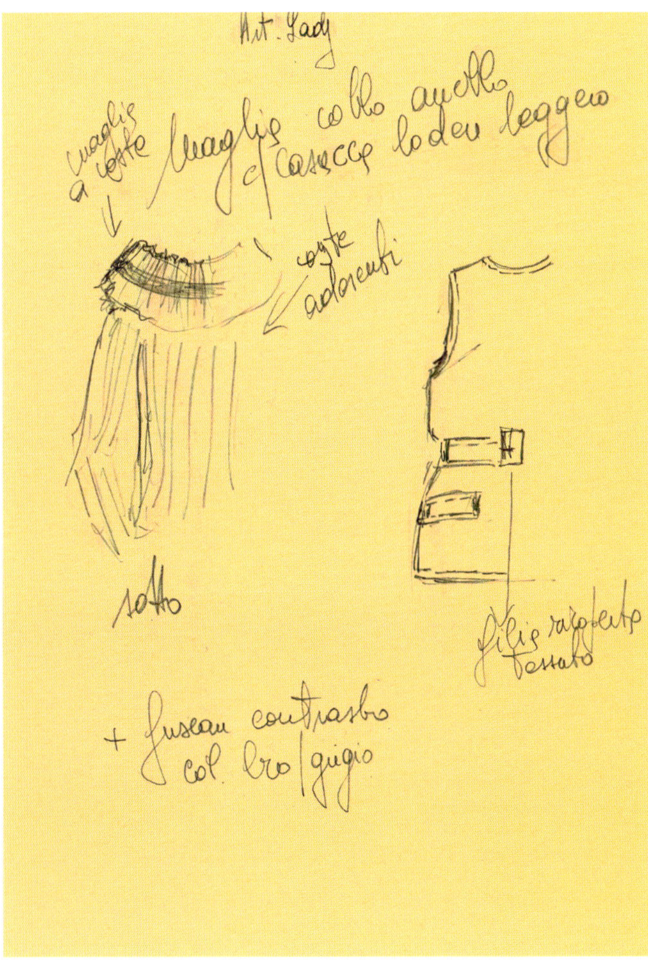

ITALO SPORT
Day suit with sleeveless jacket
c. 1959

Black and white photograph
Milan, Archivio Italo Sport

GIANPAOLA TAFFA x ITALO SPORT
Sketch for a day suit
c. 1959

Pencil on paper
Milan, Archivio Italo Sport

HANS HEITSCH
original Iceland *sweater, Igloo model*
c. 1960

Wool
Private Collection

CALZATURIFICIO DI CORNUDA "LA SCARPA MUNARI"
Master model ski boot
1956

Leather, fabric, vulcanized rubber, and small metal parts
Montebelluna, Archivio Prodotti Fondazione Sportsystem

The Master model produced by the Cornuda shoe factory "La Scarpa Munari", is one of the most significant ski boots of the mid-1950s. With this model, Austrian champion Toni Sailer won gold in three alpine skiing events at the VII Winter Olympic Games in Cortina d'Ampezzo in 1956.

Advertising campaign for original Iceland *sweaters*
c. 1960

Color print
Private Collection

UNKNOWN PHOTOGRAPHER
Ski fashion spread
1960 circa

Color print
Private Collection

The models are wearing *original Iceland* Igloo sweaters designed by Hans Heitsch and produced in Sweden for P&M Distributors, Inc. They are wearing Master ski boots produced by "La Scarpa Munari."

LA DOLOMITE
Advertisement
c. 1961

Black and white print
Courtesy Dolomite

WHITE STAG
Ski jacket
1964

Massa Lombarda, Archivi Mazzini

This garment, with Tyrolean-inspired decoration on the sleeves, was created for the 1964 Winter Olympics in Innsbruck.

DREI ZINNEN [IT] 

LA DOLOMITE
Cortina model ski boot
c. 1965

Leather, vulcanized rubber, and small metal parts
Montebelluna, Archivio Prodotti Fondazione Sportsystem

This model, probably designed for children, features one of the most important technological advances of the 1960s: metal hooks instead of laces. This not only made the boots safer, but also made it easier to control the skis.

IF THE MOUNTAINS WILL NOT COME TO FASHION, THEN FASHION WILL GO TO THE MOUNTAINS

Simona Segre-Reinach

On Tuesday, September 4, 1838, at the age of forty-four, five months, and four days—as she herself was keen to point out—Henriette d'Angeville (1794-1871), an eccentric French noblewoman living in Geneva with a passion for mountains, defied her age and gender and conquered the summit of Mont Blanc. The countess designed her own outfit for the exploit and described it in great detail in a richly illustrated diary, only published after her death and unfortunately without the illustrations, which were lost. Luckily for us, the details of her design remain: a checked wool outfit consisting of a pair of knickerbockers, a very long jacket, a long fur-lined coat adorned with a black boa, and a feathered cap as headwear. The whole outfit is said to have weighed seven or perhaps even eleven kilos. The expedition, which she led, consisted exclusively of men. In addition to provisions, their luggage included a small mirror to check for reddening of the face, eyeshades as protection from the blinding light of the glacier, and a carrier pigeon to be released at the summit to communicate the success of the mission.

Henriette's father, a French aristocrat, had been imprisoned by the revolutionaries and her grandfather guillotined. We are at the height of the revolutionary period. Having taken refuge in Switzerland, the mountaineering heroine devoted herself as much to the salons of the surviving nobility as to mountain excursions, for which she had a genuine and unwavering passion. Henriette d'Angeville was a true groundbreaker, and not just literally, because sport as we understand it today had not yet been "invented." Regulated sporting activities, very different from the physical or recreational activities that had preceded them, as historian Giorgio Riello recounts,[1] were part of the package that emerged with the new bourgeoisie of the second half of the nineteenth century; however, the presence of women in the sport was not initially envisaged.

In the mid-nineteenth century, when the famous Eng-

SLIM AARONS
Manuela Borgomanero and Emanuela Beghelli on holiday in Cortina d'Ampezzo
1976

lish tailor Charles Frederic Worth resided in Paris, *haute couture* came into being and fashion, in turn, marked the transition from aristocratic dress to that of the upper middle classes, as proposed directly by famous *couturiers* such as Frederick Worth himself, Paul Poiret, and many others. *Haute couture* was very much time-specific and directed to codified occasions in the lives of the *grandes dames*. London, on the other hand, specialized in bespoke menswear, made-to-measure by the tailors of Mayfair, and represented the counterpart to Parisian women's fashion. Modern fashion and sport are therefore contemporaries, and from the very beginning there has been crosspollination between the two worlds, despite repeated declarations of separate interests. The patriarchal culture of the time despised fashion (and women), as sociology, a disciplines also contemporary with fashion and sport, teaches us. While sport was labeled as masculine and sportswear as rational and practical, fashion was considered an expression of femininity, decorative and superfluous if not downright harmful to health. At the end of the nineteenth century, there were therefore—and still are—those who would like to consider sportswear and fashion wear as belonging to two different, almost opposite spheres, but this is not the case. Since the beginning of sporting activities, when there was no real suitable clothing and the same everyday clothes were used in the new, still élite sports such as tennis and skiing, these were practiced in a suit and tie, or in skirts in the case of women. Fashion had some influence on sport and, at the same time, elements of sportswear entered everyday life. Sportswear, especially winter sportswear, helped in the inclusion of women and the representation of different countries, as we shall see, extending the reach of fashion beyond France. Take women's trousers, for instance: Invented in the mid-nineteenth century by the American Amelia Bloomer (1818–1894), these were wide and loose-fitting and were indeed called "bloomers," designed for cycling. You could be arrested for wearing these trousers on formal occasions, as the American Helen Hulick found out in 1938 when she wore them to testify in court.[2] In the mountains, walking and skiing, not to mention trekking at high altitudes, are rather difficult if you are wearing a skirt. In the mid-nineteenth century, when skiing and mountaineering first appeared with codified rules, women who wanted to participate did so in skirts—perhaps wearing a hidden pair of trousers underneath. At the end of the nineteenth century, however, women's trousers—still problematic in urban or work contexts—were allowed in the mountains. We have seen how Henriette's outfit concealed trousers under an ample frock coat. A few years later, the first female skiers would wear divided skirts or knickerbockers beneath tunics or even under a skirt. However, when outdoor activities, especially those on the snow, ceased to be purely functional as they had been in northern Europe since ancient times, when they served only to transport goods and move people, and became a leisure activity, with mountain holidays and sporting competitions trousers became part of the female wardrobe. While fashion flourished in Paris and London, with Italy only joining in the 1950s, mountain clothing had already been cosmopolitan since the early twentieth century. The United States, a little shy in relation to Parisian *haute couture*—let us not forget Paul Poiret's electrifying "American lessons" during his American fashion tour in 1910—immediately entered the competition in winter sports clothing. The same was true for Canada, Austria, and the Nordic countries, where skiing originated. What is certain is that for both men and women, mountain clothing from the late nineteenth century until at least the 1940s was in the main heavy and bulky. Staying warm meant wearing heavy layers of wool and sweaters until the mid-1980s, with the discovery of water-repellent membranes that were applied to fabrics, the best known of which, as we shall see, is Gore-Tex. There is, therefore, a fashion in mountain clothing that is linked with the discovery of technical fabrics and that leads to specific and identifiable stages

JULES HÉBERT
Henriette d'Angeville
1838
Watercolour on paper
Private collection

WILLIAM NOTMAN
Portrait of Mme Major Lowe
1863
Silver salt print on card
Montreal, Musée McCord Stewart

AGENCE ROL
Fashion in St Moritz
1925
Print from glass negative
Paris, Bibliothèque Nationale de France

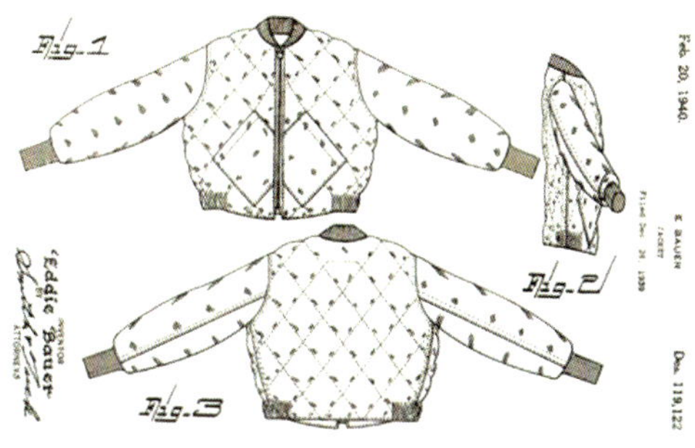

UNITED STATES PATENT OFFICE

119,122

DESIGN FOR A JACKET

Eddie Bauer, Seattle, Wash.

Application December 26, 1939, Serial No. 89,138

Term of patent 14 years

To all whom it may concern:

Be it known that I, Eddie Bauer, a citizen of the United States, residing at Seattle, in the county of King and State of Washington, have invented a new, original, and ornamental Design for a Jacket, of which the following is a specification, reference being had to the accompanying drawing forming part thereof.

Figure 1 is a front view of a jacket, showing my new design.

Figure 2 is a side view;

Figure 3 is a back view of the same.

I claim:

The ornamental design for a jacket, as shown.

EDDIE BAUER.

Fig. 1

Fig. 2

Fig. 3

Feb. 20, 1940.

Des. 119,122

Sports fashion editorial
Première neige..., *in* La Mode chic
1936

Color lithograph on paper
Paris, Bibliothèque Nationale de France

EDDIE BAUER
Patent for Blizzard Proof *jacket*
1940

Lithograph on paper
Private Collection

ITALO SPORT
Models presented at the first S. Remo Fashion Festival
1952

Black and white photograph
Milan, Archivio Italo Sport

and significant turning points. But there are also mutual influences between the two worlds of fashion and techwear, as in the so-called *après ski* clothing, a French invention that reached its peak in the 1970s. There is also a considerable exchange between the different countries that practice winter sports, making mountain clothing a global phenomenon from the very beginning.

THE 1920S

The first Winter Olympic Games, during which skiing was officially recognized as an Olympic sport, were held in 1924 in Chamonix, a town in the Haute-Savoie at the foot of Mont Blanc. The event was attended by 258 athletes from sixteen countries, with a significantly small female presence: only fourteen women were admitted, and they were limited to figure skating. However, the growing visibility of winter sports marked a turning point and in the following years an increasing number of women took up skiing, both as a sport and as a recreational activity. Woolen trousers, specifically designed for skiing, were tucked into boots and fastened with gaiters to ensure protection and comfort. Often paired with a long jacket made of the same fabric to complete the "look," they added a touch of elegance. Another significant innovation was the introduction of zip technology, which allowed for a more efficient layering of winter clothing. This improvement made skiing more accessible and comfortable both for male and female skiers, enabling them to deal more effectively with the harsh mountain temperatures.

THE 1930S

Most ski suits in the 1930s were made of heavy, warm, and durable wool, often lined with cotton flannel for added comfort. However, this decade marked an important transformation in skiwear, thanks to the introduction of new, more functional and modern materials. Among these, Lastex was particularly prominent. An innovative fabric made from rubber, it was generally treated in conjunction with rayon, cotton, or silk, thus combining strength with flexibility. It was used to create elasticated bands applied to the trouser hems and sleeve cuffs, ensuring a more snug and comfortable fit, perfect for dealing with the extreme temperatures and movement required on the slopes. At the same time, a trend appeared that added an extra touch of style: two-tone ski suits, in which jackets and trousers in contrasting colors offered a combination of elegance and practicality.
Lambswool was the main choice for skiwear until the introduction of the goose down jacket, whose invention was claimed by France in 1931 with the name *duvet* (later *doudoune*) by Pierre Allain, a mountaineer and climber, and the United States in 1936 with the Seattle brand Eddie Bauer, named after its founder. The prototype was called Blizzard Proof, with which the company obtained its first patent in 1940. The model called Skyliner is still in production. Down jackets are warm and light, and these slimmer models and warmer jackets allow skiers to move freely and remain on the slopes for longer periods. The decade also saw an increase in the popularity of baggy Norwegian trousers that are tight at the ankles, but above all of the new mountain outfits proposed by *couturiers*. Jean Patou presented his skiwear in 1930 and, in that same period, Countess Vera Borea de Buzzaccarini Regoli specialized in luxury sportswear with her Vera Borea brand. The Italian brand Italo Sport was founded in 1937 and was destined to play a leading role in the combination of winter sports and ready-to-wear fashion.
As she and her daughter Gogo loved skiing, Elsa Schiaparelli, an Italian *couturier* working in Paris, designed the ski suits that the two wore on the slopes every winter, and in 1928 added skiwear to her Pour le Sport collection. Schiaparelli experimented with new materials, innovative production processes, and functional fastenings, including visible zips and metal clips applied to the sleeves of her

EMILIO PUCCI
Mont Tremblant
1958

Printed silk twill
Como, Fondazione Antonio Ratti

WHITE STAG
Advertising campaign for the winter collection featuring prints licensed from Pablo Picasso
1963

Color print on paper
Private Collection

Cover of the house magazine Dupont Magazine
1966

Color print on paper
Private Collection

ski suits to ensure skiers stayed warm without sacrificing freedom of movement. During a trip to Norway in 1928, the Italian senator Giovanni Agnelli discovered a new sport, skiing, which was still virtually unknown in Italy. Fascinated by the sight of Norwegians gliding effortlessly over the snow-covered Scandinavian mountains, Agnelli saw the potential of the disciplines. In 1930, he purchased all the land on Colle del Sestriere, in the Cottian Alps in the province of Turin, with the aim of transforming it into a tourist resort. In 1934, Sestriere was inaugurated, a resort created from scratch with the aim of promoting and encouraging winter sports. This ambitious project put Italy on the map as an Alpine destination, encouraged the dissemination of skiing as a sport and paved the way for modern mountain tourism. Skiing also experienced an explosion in popularity in the United States between the 1930s and 1940s. On the one hand, hundreds of Austrian skiers migrated overseas after their homeland was annexed by Germany, bringing their experience with them and contributing to the popularity of the sport. On the other hand, the appeal of skiing was amplified by Hollywood movie stars, who were being photographed elegantly posed on the snow-covered slopes, transforming the sport into a symbol of glamour and style.

THE 1940S, 1950S, AND 1960S

The evolution of ski lifts allowed skiers to tackle the slopes from greater heights and with greater speed, thus leading to a significant change in skiwear. One example of this was the one-piece ski suit, characterized by a more fitted and aerodynamic design, conceived to improve performance on the slopes. It is this context that saw the emergence of Emilio Pucci, a key figure in the evolution of style on the slopes. A former Olympic skier, Pucci had competed in the 1936 Games in Garmisch, but it is with his creative intuition and his aesthetic sense that he would leave his mark. According to one account, on the slopes of Zermatt in 1947, Pucci almost accidentally designed a very modern ski suit for a friend. Photographed by Toni Frisselle and published in *Harper's Bazaar*, the image caught the attention of Diana Vreeland, editor of the magazine, thus ushering in the success of the garment. Emilio Pucci had begun his career working with Harold S. Hirsch's American company White Stag. For White Stag, he introduced the one-piece ski suit, a practical and elegant innovation that offered better protection against the elements. Pucci's jumpsuit would eventually lead to a more significant collaboration between fashion and sport and influence the very concept of functional fashion. It is worth remembering that the fashion shows organized by Giovanni Battista Giorgini in Florence in 1951 marked the birth of the modern Italian fashion industry. Rather than *haute couture*, which was in competition with its French counterpart, Florence saw the birth of Italian "boutique fashion," which was more practical and dynamic and particularly appreciated by Americans who preferred the outdoors and sportswear to the somewhat snobbish rituals of Parisian *couture*. Emilio Pucci's jumpsuit anticipated this Italo-American trend, where fashion, sport, and tourism intertwined in a new and versatile language.

A typically Milanese example is the Italian brand Italo Sport. In the late 1940s, thanks to the purchase of a batch of high-quality gabardine, the brand's inventor Italo Taffa expanded his original production of sports equipment to clothing, introducing a small tailor's workshop run by his young wife Gianpaola Tappella. Tappella, who regularly attended fashion shows in Paris, adapted French designs to the local market, as was customary at the time. The first iconic garment to become characteristic of Italo Sport's production was the hooded jacket with a front pocket, a design that is still found in sportswear today. Every winter, from the 1950s to the late 1980s, Italo Sport presented collections dedicated to life in the mountains, both for the slopes and to be worn indoors, in chalets and hotels. Italian ready-to-wear mountain wear for skiing and *après-ski* was

MISSONI
A moment from the Fall/ Winter 1971 fashion show
1971

Black and white photograph
Archivio Missoni

COLMAR
Winter fashion spread, in Sciare Moda
1977

Color print on paper
Private Collection

born. From 1948 to 1968, Italo Sport was the official brand of the Italian Olympic teams. In 1948, Maria Bogner, from the Bogner headquarters in Munich, introduced stretch trousers with stirrup straps, which immediately became all the rage. Shortly afterwards, in 1949, Klaus Obermeyer, an Austrian manufacturer and founder of Obermeyer Sport, launched a padded jacket with insulating layers and a quick-drying nylon outer shell, which marked the decline of wool as the main material for skiwear. In 1954, French mountaineer Lionel Terray, working with the Moncler brand (from Monestier-de-Clermont, a mountain village near Grenoble) on the specialist line Moncler pour Lionel Terray, explored the potential of the down jacket as techwear for hiking. That same year, the Italian expedition to Karakorum, composed of Achille Compagnoni and Lino Lacedelli, wore Moncler. Initially, Moncler down jackets were reserved for mountaineers, while Colmar windbreakers predominated in competitive downhill skiing. It was with the Colò Sheath worn by the champion skier Zeno Colò at the Oslo Olympics that Colmar (a company founded by Mario Colombo) established itself as a leading ski brand. In the 1950s, ski accessories also experienced a real boom: gloves, hats, and goggles became essential items of equipment. In particular goggles, or ski masks, became standard technical equipment, providing essential protection against the wind and the blinding glare of the snow. Finally, in 1959, a further technological revolution arrived with the introduction of Spandex (also known as Lycra or elastane), developed in the chemical laboratories of Dupont. From the 1960s onwards, the first down-filled windbreakers appeared on the ski slopes, worn over heavy sweaters, and by the end of the decade, K-way "over-trousers" were worn, as their name indicates, over trousers.

THE 1970S AND 1980S

In 1969, Italo Sport opened the first "ski market," demonstrating the growing popularity of skiing, which was now accessible even to those with no experience of high altitudes or mountaineering. Mountain clothing diversified and mixed with urban style through innovative garments such as padded nylon ski jackets with removable zipped sleeves which could be converted into waistcoats. In this climate of transformation, Giancarlo Zanatta, an entrepreneur from Montebelluna specializing in mountain boots, launched the Moon Boot, inspired by the Apollo 11 moon landing. Made of nylon, the same shape fitting both the left and right foot, and multisized, the Moon Boot quickly became an international success. Today, the Moon Boot is on display in various museums, such as New York's MoMA, the Louvre in Paris, and the Triennale Design Museum in Milan. "Official" fashion continued to design for the mountains, as demonstrated by Pierre Cardin's ski collections in the early 1970s, which were characterized by futuristic goggles and space-inspired details. This same trend was maintained by all future designers.

In March 1971, Missoni presented a women's Après-ski collection in Cortina: a total look of plain knitted outfits with multicoloured patchwork inserts. The newspapers began to compare Ottavio and Rosita Missoni's colour combinations to works of contemporary art. In 1976, another revolution took place with the invention of Gore-Tex, a waterproof and breathable membrane applied to windproof fabrics, designed by the husband-and-wife team Wilbert and Geneviève Gore, who had left Dupont. Gore was already being used in the engineering, space, and medical fields, but its application in that of textiles, with the heat-sealing patented in 1979, completely revolutionized mountain clothing, making it lighter and more practical.

The 1980s brought a breath of color and boldness to the slopes, where skiers sported lightweight suits in fluorescent neon shades, paired with bright accessories such as headbands and sunglasses in vibrant colors. Icons of this style included Princess Diana, photographed in Klosters in 1986 wearing a fiery red jumpsuit and a headband, and

Princess Hanau Schambger, photographed in her chalet in Gstaad in 1985, comfortably reclining on a sofa with a glass of champagne in her hand and voluminous fur Moon Boots on her feet. This maximalist aesthetic defined the era, expressing a carefree and opulent vision of the mountains. Meanwhile, the introduction of synthetic fleece fabric transformed the way people dressed, allowing skiers to adopt a more efficient and versatile layering system. Canadian brands, such as Sorel and Canada Goose, also began to integrate ski aesthetics into everyday streetwear. In Milan, the Paninari, a subculture of young, fashion-conscious hedonists, converted the Moncler down jacket into an iconic urban garment, bringing techwear down from the mountains to the streets of the city, in a combination of functionality and style that marked an era.

FROM THE 1990S TO THE PRESENT

From the 1990s and 2000s was a period of continuous technological innovation for skiwear. Fabrics became increasingly advanced, with significant improvements in waterproofing, breathability, and durability, while high-performance materials such as synthetic insulation became the new standard. Leather ski boots with cotton laces gave way to plastic models with hook fastenings, which were more practical and efficient. The growing popularity of snowboarding also had a profound influence on the aesthetics of skiing: wide trousers, graphic prints, and oversized jackets became the norm, marking a break with the more fitted look of the recent past. In addition, logos and brands took center stage, transforming skiwear into a statement of style and identity. Meanwhile, neon shades gave way to a more delicate palette dominated by pastel colors. Ski helmets, initially designed as essential safety accessories, become elements of style to stand out on the slopes or when mountain climbing, such as those by Salewa, the Bolzano-based company. Moncler, acquired by Remo Ruffini in 2006, established itself as a high-end fashion brand with its down jackets. The brand consolidated its international stature thanks to continuous technical innovations and sophisticated designs. The 2020s saw a flourishing of collaborations and cocreations. Some examples include Pucci x Fusalp, Chloè x Fusalp, and Moncler Genius X Willow Smith, inspired by science fiction. Loro Piana announced a luxury line for 2025 called Aprèsski, characterized by the innovative use of traditional materials such as reversed sheepskin, jacquard cashmere, *Cashfur*, and *Pecora Nera*.
With the growing awareness of environmental issues, many companies now prefer to use recycled or responsibly sourced materials. These companies include Patagonia, long a symbol of sustainability in the outdoor sector. At the same time, increasing public awareness and sensitivity to animal welfare have prompted companies to review their production chains to reduce their impact on the environment and become cruelty-free. The elegant "down jackets" by Shoreditch Ski Club are made from recycled plastic bottles, including the lining and padding, thus completely eliminating the use of animal feathers, a growing trend in the sector and following in the footsteps of pioneer Save the Duck. Perfect Moment, loved by celebrities and influencers, combines an ironic retro aesthetic with a strong focus on functionality. Founded by Thierry Donard, a documentary filmmaker specializing in extreme sports, the brand subjects each garment to specific tests before putting it on the market. Messy-Weekend, based in Copenhagen, stands out for its production of ski goggles and sunglasses that are characterized by minimalist design and advanced technology, such as high-contrast lenses with UV400 protection. The brand's environmental commitment is reflected in its commitment to ocean cleanup initiatives, where plastic is removed from the oceans with every purchase. In the name of a sustainable social group, design, and accessibility, Italian Olympic champion Deborah Compagnoni

KWAY
Winter fashion spread,
in Sciare. L'annuario della Moda Sci
1978

Color print on paper
Private Collection

MONCLER
Advertising campaign
1982

Color print on paper
Private Collection

THE NORTH FACE x MM6
Down jacket
2020

Private Collection

CHLOÉ* x *FUSALP
Ski suit
2020

Courtesy Fusalp

OFF-WHITE
View of the Fall/Winter 2021 collection in collaboration with Arc'teryx
2020

CANADA GOOSE* x *KIDSUPER
Down jacket
2024

Private Collection

launched the Altavia by Deborah Compagnoni line in 2024 in collaboration with OVS.

What has always been merely an apparent separation between the two worlds is now definitely no longer the case. On the one hand, we have Virgil Abloh's Off-White Fall/Winter 2021 fashion collection, in which models shared the catwalk with athletes, introducing the fashion-conscious public to one of the most technical and highly regarded brands in the outdoor world, and on the other, the Canadian brand Arc'teryx, with vintage fashion that reinterprets 1970s and 1980s ski gear in a "fashionable" way, such as the PostCard brand in Ridley Scott's film *The House of Gucci*.

These examples reaffirm how fashion and techwear have always gone hand in hand and influenced each other. In the historical continuity of this interaction, we can say that functionality has constantly shaped style and vice versa. Today, the marriage of technical performance and aesthetic sensibility manifests itself in new forms and confirms that mountain wear and outdoor clothing has never just been a question of functionality, but also an expression of identity and style.

[1] Giorgio Riello, *La moda*, Laterza, Rome Bari 2021.
[2] It should be borne in mind that girls were not allowed to wear trousers to school in Italy until the late 1950s.

BILL WOGGON
Katy in Skating Fashions, in Katy Keene, no. 57
January 1961

Color lithograph on card
Private Collection

BILL WOGGON
Debby's Duds, in Katy Keene, no. 57
January 1961

Color lithograph on card
Private Collection

CARL IWASAKI
Batman and Robin
1966

Color print
Private Collection

Ski instructor Roger Staub (left) and patrol member Chuck Malloy (right) speed down the slopes of Vail, Colorado, dressed as Batman and Robin.

MAC RABOY
Captain Marvel Jr. in Ski Jump
1944

Color lithograph on card
Private Collection

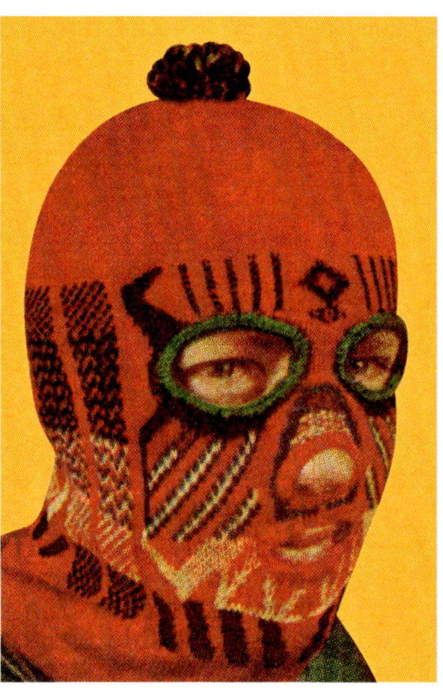

UNKNOWN PHOTOGRAPHER
Balaclava models
c. 1960

Color print

Series of photographs used for Italian and French fashion magazine articles on balaclavas.

UNKNOWN PHOTOGRAPHER
Two skiers wearing balaclavas
1962

Color print

Created as a piece of military clothing during the Crimean War (1854), the balaclava takes its name from the Ukrainian city where a famous battle took place, and was used to protect British troops from the cold. Subsequently, this knitted head covering has been used in many different contexts—from political activism to urban clothing—eventually becoming part of the technical equipment for winter sports. Thanks to the protection it affords against wind and frost, the balaclava has established itself as an essential accessory for skiing and other outdoor disciplines, and has evolved into an object of fashion and stylistic experimentation.

BLIZZARD
Study for the Logo
1962

Color print
Courtesy Tecnica Group

Erfolgreichster Ski
der Alpinen Skiweltmeisterschaft 1962
in Chamonix!

Weltmeister in Abfahrt, Slalom und Riesentorlauf!

3mal Gold
2mal Silber
2mal Bronze
bei den Alpinen
Skiweltmeisterschaften
in Chamonix!

BLIZZARD
BLIZZARD-SKI

BLIZZARD
Advertising campaign
1962

Color print
Courtesy Tecnica Group

Founded in 1945 by Anton Arnsteiner in Mittersill at the foot of the Austrian Alps, Blizzard has made skiing history with its pioneering approach to technology and materials. From the first polyethylene base to metal and fiberglass, the brand has been at the forefront of modern skiing. In 1962, Christl Haas, Erika Netzer, and Marianne Jahn achieved a historic triple victory at the World Championships in Chamonix on Blizzard skis, also winning silver in the giant slalom with the Epoxi model.

Sophia Loren on the ice rink
1965

Gina Lollobrigida skiing
1962

Brigitte Bardot on skis
1967

Monochrome print on paper
Private Collection

Spreads from Japanese magazines in the 1960s, all related to the theme of movie stars enjoying themselves in the snow.

UNKNOWN PHOTOGRAPHER
Audrey Hepburn in Charade
1963

Color print
Private Collection

Filmed in 1963, Stanley Donen's *Charade* combines suspense, comedy, and romance against the backdrop of an iconic Paris. But it is in the scenes set in Megève, an elegant ski resort at the foot of Mont Blanc, that the film establishes an unprecedented link with winter sports. To shoot these scenes, the cast and crew of about sixty people moved to the mountains and needed twelve trucks to transport complex technical equipment. Filming in the snow, with alpine landscapes as a natural backdrop, combined cinematic glamour and ski culture, helping to cement the elegant image of winter holidays in the French Alps. Audrey Hepburn, well known for her close collaboration with fashion designer Hubert de Givenchy, also wears outfits by the French couturier in *Charade*.

雪を楽しむ

Brigitte BARDOT

IT'S SNOWING!

ITALIAN MANUFACTURE
Quilted jacket
c. 1965

Massa Lombarda, Archivi Mazzini

MICHÈLE ROSIER POUR V DE V
Quilted ski suit
c. 1965

Massa Lombarda, Archivi Mazzini

THE PALA GROUP [IT]

LAHCO SNOWY LOOK
Lightly padded stretch nylon windbreakers with waxed finish
1966

Color print
Private Collection

ARNAUD DE ROSNAY
Spread on winter fashions in Vogue
November 1, 1968

Color print
Private Collection

The model is wearing quilted trousers and a jacket with a hood, all by Michèle Rosier pour V de V, and goggles by Bernard Kayman.

DOLOMITE
Flying Kilometer *boot*
1966

Vulcanized rubber, metal parts
Montebelluna, Archivio Prodotti Fondazione Sportsystem

Ski boot for the "flying kilometer" (a skiing discipline that consists of descending a steep slope to reach maximum speed, measured at the lowest point of the slope over a timed 100-meter stretch), developed in collaboration with the Finnish champion Kalevi Hakkinen. Wearing these boots, Hakkinen reached a speed of 172.331 km/h in Cervinia in 1968.

LANGE
Ski boot
1962

Plastic material
Montebelluna, Archivio Prodotti Fondazione Sportsystem

This is probably the first plastic ski boot ever produced. It was made by Lange, who molded the boot in two separate parts. It was released on the market in limited numbers.

TONI FRISSELL
Suzy Chaffee on the slopes of Vail, Colorado
1969

Color print
Washington D.C., Library of Congress

American skier Suzy Chaffee joined the national team in 1965, finishing fifth in the downhill at the 1966 World Championships, and distinguishing herself in the World Cup between 1966 and 1967. She went on to become a leading figure in freestyle skiing, winning the unofficial ballet championships three years in a row (1971–1973).
A pop culture icon, Chaffee captured the media's attention with a silver racing suit worn at the 1968 Winter Olympics in Grenoble and later with a series of advertising campaigns, including one for the ChapStick brand, which earned her the nickname Suzy Chapstick. A model for Vogue and represented by the Ford agency, she combined her sporting and modeling career with a strong civic commitment: a member of the United States Olympic Committee and the President's Council on Physical Fitness, in 1996 she cofounded the Native Voices Foundation to support Native American athletes' access to Olympic competitions.

Considered to be one of the pioneers of American sportswear, Bonnie Cashin redefined women's clothing in the postwar period, emphasizing functionality, freedom of movement, and everyday practicality. After starting out in costume design for theater and film, she developed a distinctive stylistic language based on clean lines, technical materials, and modular overlays. Throughout her career, she introduced innovations such as "layering pieces" and iconic metal turnlock fasteners, which were later adopted by Coach, for whom she was a designer from the 1960s onwards. Her idea of sportswear transcended performance in the strict sense of the term: for Cashin, it meant creating clothes that responded to the needs of the dynamic, independent, and modern woman. Her vision contributed significantly to defining the identity of American style in the second half of the twentieth century.

COURRÈGES
Ski outfit: waistcoat and skirt
c. 1965

Massa Lombarda, Archivi Mazzini

HIPERBOLE. COURRÈGES PARIS
After-ski outfit: waistcoat and trousers
c. 1965

Massa Lombarda, Archivi Mazzini

 GSTAAD [CH]

BONNIE CASHIN
Sketch for an outfit with heaGDRess and miniskirt
1966

BONNIE CASHIN
Sketch for outfit with cape
1966

BONNIE CASHIN
Sketch for a hooded sweater and mini-dress ensemble
1966

BONNIE CASHIN
Sketch for outfit with overlapping capes
1966

Pencil and pastels on paper
Los Angeles, UCLA, Library Special Collections, Charles E. Young Research Library

ROSSIGNOL
Advertising campaign
1971

Color print
Photo Archivio Rossignol

UNKNOWN PHOTOGRAPHER
Emile Allais and Adrien Duvillard driving two DS with Rossignol advertising silhouettes on the bonnet
c. 1960

Color print
Photo Archivio Rossignol

Emile Allais and Adrien Duvillard wrote fundamental chapters in French skiing history: the former was three-time gold medallist at the 1937 World Championships in Chamonix and innovator of the French method; the latter was a versatile and tenacious athlete who narrowly missed out on an Olympic medal in Cortina, and won on historic slopes such as the Streif. Both were not only users of but also consultants for Rossignol skis. Emile Allais contributed to the creation of the Olympic 41, the Métaillais, and the Allais 60.

CORGI TOYS
Citroen ID 19 Safari, special edition of the Grenoble Olympiade 1968
1968

Tin, plastic, and rubber
Private Collection

CALZE GM
Box for socks by Calze GM Sport *catalogue*
c. 1970

Color print
Courtesy Calze GM

Founded in 1959 in Trento by Giorgio Montagni, Calze GM, although its initial product was fishnet stockings, immediately focused on sports thanks to the introduction of the first Bentley machines, becoming the supplier of the Italian national alpine skiing team in the 1970s. Over time, GM products accompanied athletes and sports stars such as Franco Nones, Gustav Thöni, Piero Gros, Erwin Stricker, Francesco Moser, Alberto Tomba, the Ragni di Lecco mountaineers, and Reinhold Messner.

COLMAR
Wool padded jacket
c. 1970

ELLESSE
Ski trousers
c. 1970

ANBA OF AUSTRIA
Ski suit
c. 1970

Massa Lombarda, Archivi Mazzini

MATTERHORN [IT] 

CALZE GM
Pages from the Calzificio G.M. *catalogue*
1967

Color print
Courtesy Calze GM

In 1968, Calze GM was the official supplier to the Italian national team at the Winter Olympics in Grenoble. On February 7, in Autrans, Franco Nones won the 30-km cross-country skiing event. In the lead from the first 500 meters, he maintained his advantage over Mäntyranta and Martinsen, finishing more than 50 seconds ahead of the runner-up. It was the first non-Scandinavian Olympic gold medal in the discipline. Italy also saw De Florian finish in fifth place. Franco Nones went on to become an ambassador for Calze GM.

OTTAVIO AND ROSITA MISSONI
Après-ski collection: detail of a patchwork knitwear garment
1971

Wool
Archivio Missoni

BRUNETTA
Illustration for the Missoni collection
1971

Ink on paper
Archivio Missoni

Brunetta's illustration depicts the first patchwork garments that the Missonis designed for the Après-ski collection, showcased in March 1971 in Cortina.

TECNICA
Advertising campaign for Tecnus boots by Tecnica
1972

Color print
Courtesy Tecnica Group

TECNICA
Advertising campaign for Moon Boot by Tecnica
1972

Color print
Courtesy Tecnica Group

From the crafts workshop founded in 1930 by Oreste Zanatta, the Tecnica shoe factory was established in Montebelluna in 1960 and headed by Zanatta's son Giancarlo. The company conquered the international market with two iconic innovations: Moon Boots, launched in 1969 with their space-age aesthetic; and Tecnus, the first bi-injected plastic ski boot, introduced in 1970.

TECNICA
Moon Boot
c. 1970

Massa Lombarda, Archivi Mazzini

ROSSIGNOL
ROC 550
1971

Photo Archivio Rossignol

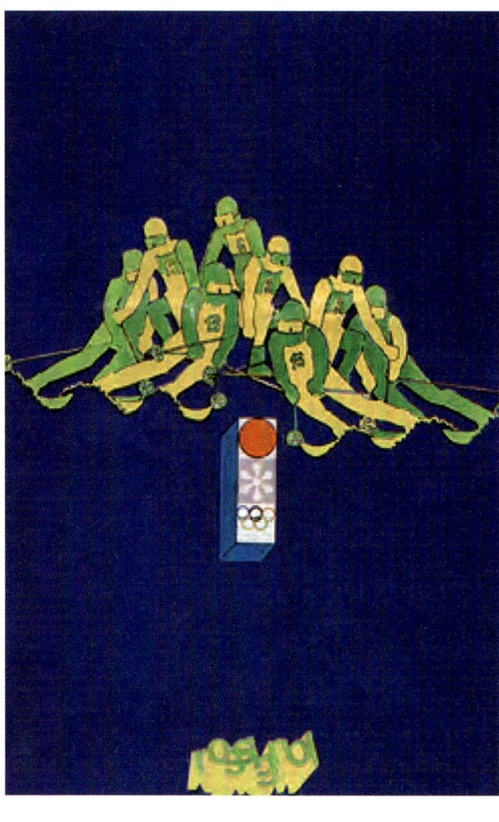

ROSSIGNOL
Advertising campaign
1972

ROSSIGNOL
Advertising campaign for the 1972 Olympic Games in Sapporo
1972

Color print
Photo Archivio Rossignol

ROSSIGNOL
Cover of the 72/73 catalogue
1972

Color print
Photo Archivio Rossignol

DOLOMITEN
Ski sweater
c. 1970

ROSSIGNOL
Ski sweater
c. 1970

Massa Lombarda, Archivi Mazzini

WEISSHORN [CH]

DOLOMITEN
R

DINO F.LLI BERTELÈ
Ski boot
1973

Aluminum and polyurethane
Montebelluna, Archivio Prodotti Fondazione Sportsystem

Ski boot with aluminum and polyurethane shell. A distinctive feature of this model is the upward opening of the front part of the shell, thanks to the presence of a hinge on the toe of the boot.

LEVI'S
Advertising campaign for snow trousers
c. 1975

Color print
Private Collection

GIGI RIZZI
Advertising campaign
1977

Color print
Private Collection

VÀLIMON
Advertising page for padded waterproof jeans
1973

Color print
Milan, Archivio Italo Sport

FILA
Ski jacket
c. 1970

FILA
Ski jacket
c. 1970

Massa Lombarda, Archivi Mazzini

GARMONT
Aesthetic proposal for a ski boot
1974

Wood and plaster
Montebelluna, Archivio Prodotti Fondazione Sportsystem

Model for a ski boot created through the collaboration between the Pininfarina design studio and the Garmont company. It is the aesthetic model for this ski boot that is published here, that is a 1:1 full scale example that allows the product to be viewed preproduction in its size, shape, and colors.

DOLOMITE
RA CLAYTON

ELLESSE
Ski jacket
c. 1970

Massa Lombarda, Archivi Mazzini

ELLESSE
Ski jacket
c. 1970

Massa Lombarda, Archivi Mazzini

ELLESSE
Ski jacket
c. 1970

Massa Lombarda, Archivi Mazzini

PIERRE CARDIN
Ski jacket
c. 1970

Massa Lombarda, Archivi Mazzini

DOLOMITE
Advertising campaign
c. 1970

Color print
Courtesy Dolomite

PIERRE CARDIN
Ski jacket
c. 1970

Massa Lombarda, Archivi Mazzini

VÀLIMON x ITALO SPORT
Ski fashion spread
1973–1975

Color print
Milan, Archivio Italo Sport

SALVATORE FERRAGAMO
Skier
Fall/Winter 1977

Silk crepe
Florence, Museo Ferragamo

FUSALP
Ski jacket
c. 1970

Courtesy Fusalp

FUSALP
Ski jacket
c. 1970

Courtesy Fusalp

FUSALP
Ski jacket
c. 1990

Courtesy Fusalp

FUSALP
Ski suit
Christine Rossi
c. 1980

Courtesy Fusalp

Founded in Annecy in 1952 by Georges Ribola and René Veyrat, Fusalp—an acronym for Fuseau des Alpes—radically transformed skiwear by introducing technical, stretch-fit ski pants and, in 1966, the first racing suit at the World Championships in Portillo. The following decade marked the brand's creative peak: with Ingrid Buchner as artistic director and Nadine Portigliati in charge of material development, Fusalp conquered the slopes and the city, blending style and performance in an unprecedented way. The modern silhouettes and cutting-edge materials became symbols of a typically French sporting elegance. In the 1980s, the freestyle champion Christine Rossi launched a long collaboration with Fusalp with a bespoke ski suit developed together with designer Nadine Portigliati, designed to enhance movement and aesthetics in competition.

JAN SØDERSTRØM, TOVE KJÆR
Hat from the 1982 Nordic World Ski Championships in Oslo
1982

Wool
Oslo, Nasjonalmuseet

ELLEN LOVISA ELG
Wool hat for festive celebrations in Vikmanshyttan
1981

Wool
Falun, Dalarnas museum

KOCKARGÅRDENS HEMSLÖJD
Tällberg hat
1980

Wool
Falun, Dalarnas museum

UNN SØILAND DALE x MAISON DIOR
Dress
c. 1980

Wool
Oslo, Nasjonalmuseet

HAGLEBU [NO]

INGER OHLSSON
Söderbärk hat
1980–1981

Wool
Falun, Dalarnas museum

SÖDRA DALARNAS HEMSLÖJDSFÖRENING
Hedemoramössan
1980–1981

Wool
Falun, Dalarnas museum

NORDICA
Cover of the Nordica 82-83 *catalogue*
1982

Color print
Courtesy Tecnica Group

The photograph on the cover shows the three different colors of the Trident model.

UNKNOWN MANUFACTURE

Ski boot mold

c. 1980

Wood and resin
Montebelluna, Archivio Prodotti Fondazione Sportsystem

Part of the process of studying and developing a new ski boot model involved creating what is known as a "mosaic." This is a representation of the various components of the new ski boot made out of pieces of wood and resin, necessary in order to check thickness and measurements before proceeding with the creation of the molds for mass production.

NORDICA

Ski boot model

c. 1980

Wood, resin, and plaster
Montebelluna,
Archivio Prodotti Fondazione Sportsystem

Model for a ski boot made of wood and plaster using the "mosaic" technique. It consists of two parts: the interior and exterior faces of the ski boot. The creation of such models was one of the fundamental steps in the subsequent production of molds for the manufacture of ski boots.

UNKNOWN MANUFACTURE

Ski boot shell

c. 1980

Leather
Montebelluna,
Archivio Prodotti Fondazione Sportsystem

COLMAR
Padded snow jacket
c. 1980

BELFE
Sweater, sleeveless padded snow jacket, and trousers
c. 1980

Massa Lombarda, Archivi Mazzini

ISCHL [AT]

SWATCH
POP Swatch Jet Black
POP Swatch Fire Signal
POP Swatch Blue Ribbon
1986

Courtesy Swatch

In 1986, Swatch launched the POP collection. In a subsequent evolution, the brand integrated a technical feature into the collection for the first time—the RECCO® system, which was designed to locate people buried in an avalanche.

ALAN RANDALL BEST
Blue speed skiing helmet
1985-1986

Fiberglass, hand-laminated polyester resin, acrylic paint, high-density impact-resistant foam, velvet, and polycarbonate filter
New York, The Museum of Modern Art

KEVAN LAYCRAFT
ALAN RANDALL BEST
Red speed skiing helmet
1981

Fiberglass and plastic
New York, The Museum of Modern Art

COLMAR
belfe

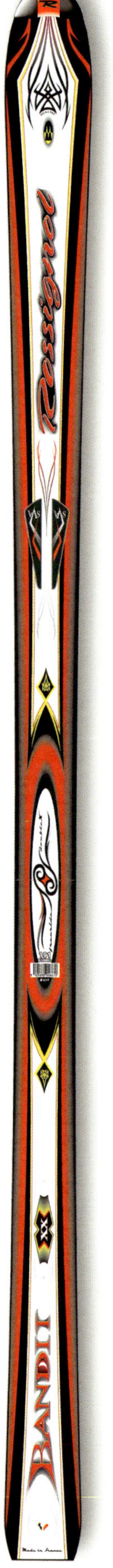

ROSSIGNOL
4S
(detail and overall view)
1987

ROSSIGNOL
7S
1992

ROSSIGNOL
Bandit
1999

Photo Archivio Rossignol

The 4S skis defined an era—with over a million pairs sold worldwide—and were the co-stars of several World Cup victories and at the 1988 Olympic Games in Calgary, with Alberto Tomba, Erica Hess, Vreni Schneider, and Rok Petrovic.

MONCLER
Men's down jacket
c. 1980

MONCLER
Women's down jacket
c. 1980

Massa Lombarda, Archivi Mazzini

PANEVEGGIO [IT] 

MONCLER
MONCLER

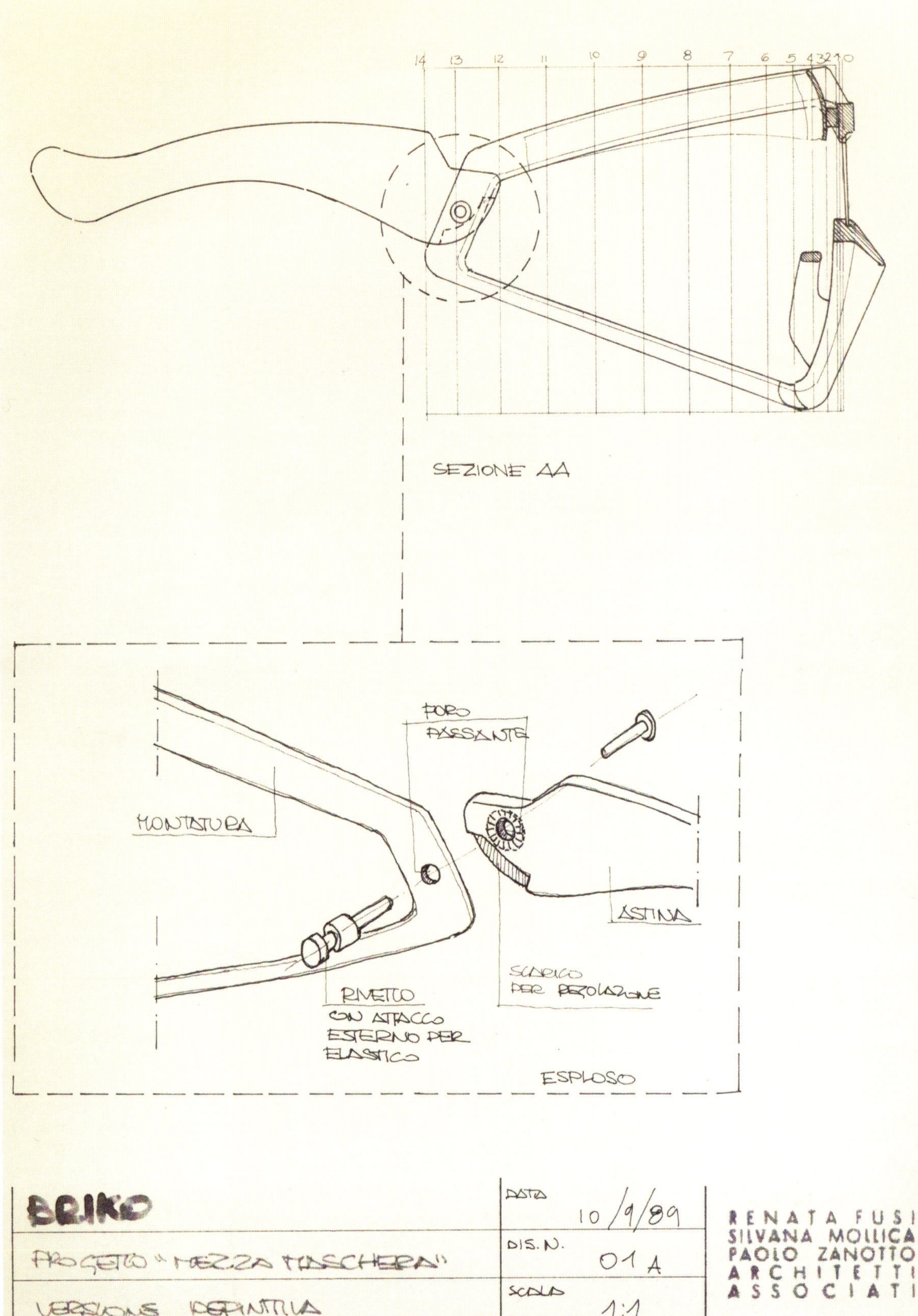

RENATA FUSI, SILVANA MOLLICA, PAOLO ZANOTTO ARCHITETTI ASSOCIATI x BRIKO
Detector. Technical drawing of the detail of the fastening system of the mask and the temples
1989

Pencil and felt-tip on paper
Courtesy Archivio Renata Fusi, Silvana Mollica, Paolo Zanotto Architetti Associati

Designed by Renata Fusi, Silvana Mollica, and Paolo Zanotto for Briko, Detector is a technical multisport model developed to combine the characteristics of a ski mask and sports goggles, designed to adapt to different sports from skiing to paragliding, hang gliding, snowboarding, and cycling. The design allows for a wide field of vision, including side vision, while the aluminum frame protects against impact. The use of PVC and foam materials in the temples, nose bridge, and brow bar ensures comfort and adaptability to different face shapes.

The modular attachment system allows the glasses to be quickly transformed according to the desired use: from sports glasses to ski goggles and city glasses, thanks to the interchangeable rigid temples and elastic headband.

Winner of the Compasso d'Oro award in 1991, with the following statement from the jury: "for the extreme rigor that combines the ductility of the material with its functional use."

RENATA FUSI, SILVANA MOLLICA, PAOLO ZANOTTO ARCHITETTI ASSOCIATI x BRIKO
The different parts of the Detector ski goggles
1991

Courtesy Archivio Renata Fusi, Silvana Mollica, Paolo Zanotto Architetti Associati

RENATA FUSI, SILVANA MOLLICA, PAOLO ZANOTTO ARCHITETTI ASSOCIATI x BRIKO
Detector ski goggles
1991

Courtesy Archivio Renata Fusi, Silvana Mollica, Paolo Zanotto Architetti Associati

Team 85451

Team 85501

Rocket 85551

Rocket 85601

Rocket 85651

Rocket 85701

Detector silver 85201

Detector blue 85251

RENATA FUSI, SILVANA MOLLICA, PAOLO ZANOTTO ARCHITETTI ASSOCIATI x BRIKO

Pages from the 1992 Briko catalogue displaying the Team, Rocket, and Detector models

1992

Color print

Courtesy Archivio Renata Fusi, Silvana Mollica, Paolo Zanotto Architetti Associati

Performance and aesthetics become essential elements of design for advertising in the 1990s. The choice of color becomes increasingly important, not only to characterize products and lines, but also to make products identifiable on the ski slopes at a time when the sponsorship of athletes had not yet been made official.

SERGIO TACCHINI

Ski suit

c. 1985

Milan, Archivio Ricciuti

ISSEY MIYAKE

Ski suit

c. 1985

YOHJI YAMAMOTO

Wool hat and gloves

c. 1990

Massa Lombarda, Archivi Mazzini

GHIACCIAIO TASMAN [NZ] 

LA PLOSE 1991

TROFEO

1/30 Missoni 91

FILA SPRINT

GLADYS PERINT PALMER
Illustrations for the Missoni Women's Collection
1992

Felt-tip pens on paper
Archivio Missoni

OTTAVIO MISSONI
La plose 1991. Trofeo Fila Sprint
1991

Lithograph on paper
Archivio Missoni

OTTAVIO AND ROSITA MISSONI
Detail of a jacquard knitted fabric in boiled wool
Fall/Winter 1992

Printed fabric
Archivio Missoni

OTTAVIO AND ROSITA MISSONI
Hooded capes
Fall/Winter 1992

Wool
Archivio Missoni

MONTE TOMBA [IT]

YASUHIKO KOBAYASHI x SKIER
Cover illustration for SKIER, no. 1
1993

© Yasuhiko Kobayashi / SKIER Magazine, Yama to Keikoku Sha

YASUHIKO KOBAYASHI x SKIER
Cover illustration for SKIER, no. 6
1991

© Yasuhiko Kobayashi / SKIER Magazine, Yama to Keikoku Sha

YASUHIKO KOBAYASHI x SKIER
Cover illustration for SKIER, no. 2
1993

© Yasuhiko Kobayashi / SKIER Magazine, Yama to Keikoku Sha

YASUHIKO KOBAYASHI x SKIER
Cover illustration for SKIER, no. 4
1993

© Yasuhiko Kobayashi / SKIER Magazine, Yama to Keikoku Sha

YASUHIKO KOBAYASHI x SKIER
Cover illustration for SKIER, no. 4
1984

© Yasuhiko Kobayashi / SKIER Magazine, Yama to Keikoku Sha

Between 1979 and 1995, Yasuhiko Kobayashi created around a hundred covers for the Japanese magazine *SKIER*, published by Yama to Keikoku Sha, becoming one of the most recognizable visual voices of the skiing boom in Japan. Over this period, between the rise of ski culture in the 1980s and the peak of the Japanese economic bubble in the early 1990s, skiing established itself as a social phenomenon and symbol of youth lifestyle. Kobayashi's illustrations, characterized by a vivid narrative style, reflect and document the aesthetics and energy of that era, becoming visual witnesses to the transformation of skiing into a cultural phenomenon.

別冊付録
1 日本のスキー学校303
2 スキー少年・少女新聞"SKI BOY'S PRESS"
3 スキー・サジェッション コラム93

特集 楽しきは合宿

skierは，合宿とは「複数の人間が同じ場所にステイして同じ釜の飯を食う行為」と拡大解釈します。となればスキーそのものが合宿なのでありますね。この場合，合コンとか合ハイといった軽〜い感じの合宿(ゴーシュク)というのをすすめます。スキーはすべて楽しい合宿，というわけで合宿HOW TO特集

付録共·定価1000円

特別研究 スキー・ザッツ・マネー

スキーって高いか安いかもうかるか，こうすりゃソンするトクをする……のお金にまつわる話すべて

技術特集 どうすればうまくなるかの方程式

どうすれば早く，しかも効率的にうまくなれるのか。これを徹底的に考え，その答えをだしました

Yes! happiness, Ski story of USA

海外レポート——アメリカン・スキーストーリー

アスペンに住む7人のスキーフリークの生活。そして，ガイド・ストーリー[アスペンVSレイクタホ]

skier '84·NO.4
特集 楽しきは合宿
別冊付録 日本のスキー学校303
山と溪谷社

GIANNI VERSACE
Women's suit:
padded jacket and lace skirt
Fall/Winter 1996

Private Collection

ŠAR MOUNTAINS [MK]

ANDY WARHOL
Frölunda Hockey Player
1986

ANDY WARHOL
Frölunda Hockey Player
1986

Color silkscreen print on
Lenox Museum Board
Private Collection

ANDY WARHOL
Frölunda Hockey Player
1986

Color silkscreen print on
Lenox Museum Board
Private Collection

RENATA FUSI, SILVANA MOLLICA, PAOLO ZANOTTO ARCHITETTI ASSOCIATI x BRIKO
Study sketch for B-Zone sunglasses
1994

Pencil and felt-tip pen on paper
Courtesy Archivio Renata Fusi, Silvana Mollica, Paolo Zanotto Architetti Associati

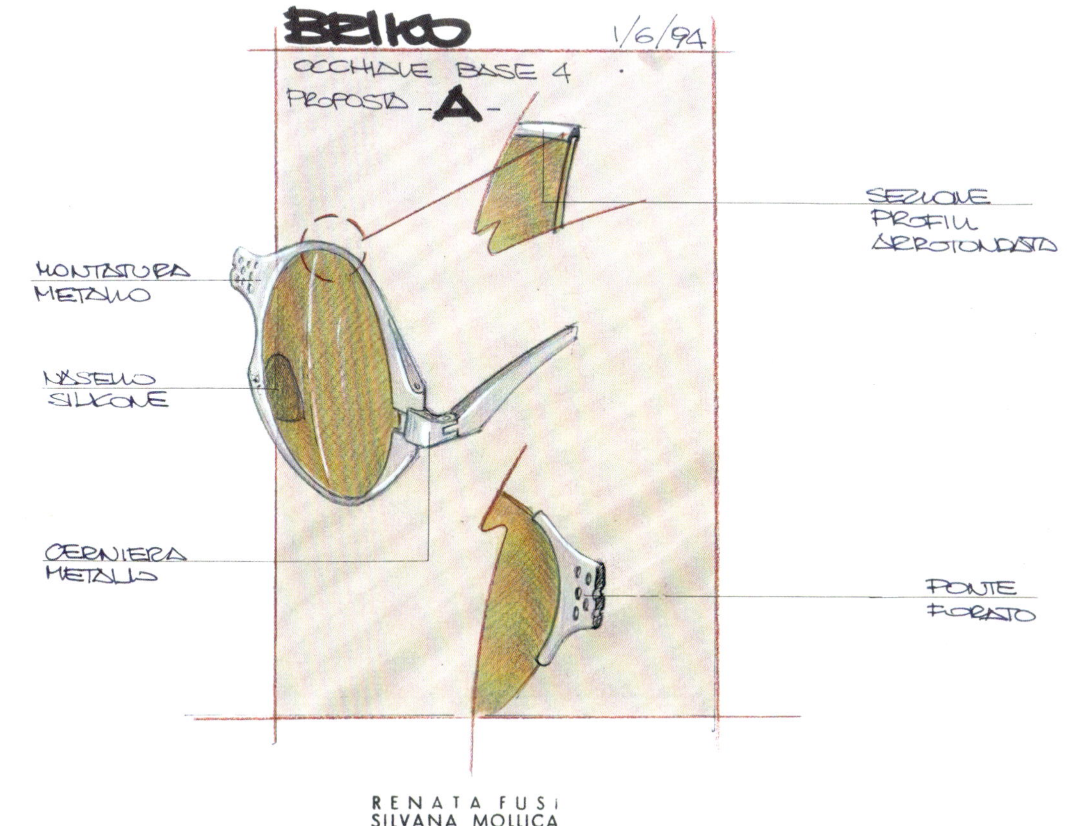

HELMUT LANG
Men's suit: padded jacket and trousers
Fall/Winter 1992

HELMUT LANG
Women's suit: padded jacket and skirt
Fall/Winter 1992

Massa Lombarda, Archivi Mazzini

MONT BLANC [IT]

RENATA FUSI, SILVANA MOLLICA, PAOLO ZANOTTO ARCHITETTI ASSOCIATI x BRIKO
B-Zone sunglasses
1994

Metal foil and plastic material
Courtesy Archivio Renata Fusi, Silvana Mollica, Paolo Zanotto Architetti Associati

Made from an ultra-light metal alloy, the B-Zone line models have been designed to meet both high sporting performance requirements (for winter sports and cycling) and a more urban aesthetic. The design of the glasses can be distinguished by its ultra-flat profile, achieved through the use of metal foil. The lenses are mounted using patented Flush Glass technology, which minimizes the thickness of the frame. The adjustable nose pads and temple tips are made of DuPont Hytrel®, a material chosen for its comfort and stability.

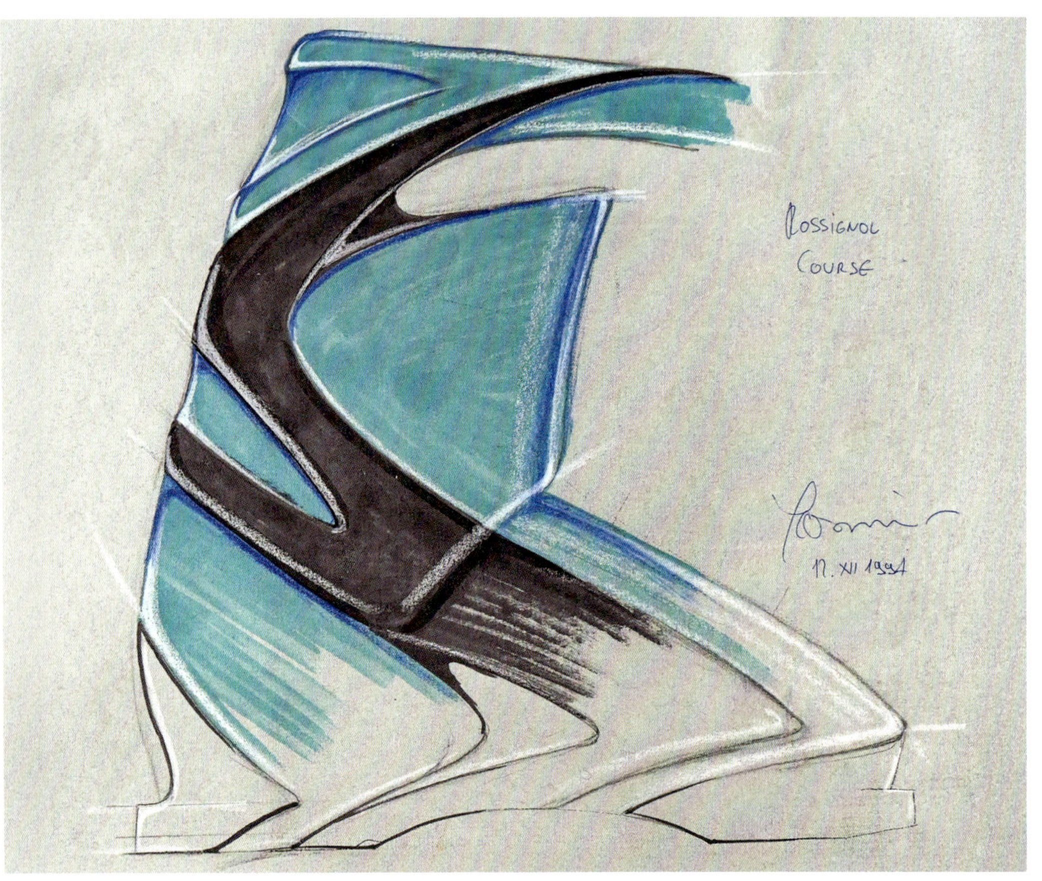

JASMINA KALUDEROVIC x ROSSIGNOL

Snowboard boot, Freestyle model

1995

JASMINA KALUDEROVIC x ROSSIGNOL

Snowboard boot, Freestyle model

1995

JASMINA KALUDEROVIC x ROSSIGNOL

Study sketches for Freestyle snowboard boots

1995

Mixed media rendering:
Pantone and colored pencils on paper
Courtesy Jasmina Kaluderovic

Designed to combine the comfort of a soft structure with the performance of a rigid snowboard boot, the Freestyle model is one of the first examples of crosshybridization between fashion and technical footwear for winter sports. Made from a denim-like fabric, a fabric previously unheard of in the sector, the boot marked a turning point in the aesthetics of technical footwear. The Freestyle model was designed to combine the comfort of a soft structure with the performance of a hard shoe, traditionally made of plastic.
A distinctive feature is the sole, designed to wrap around the foot and improve stability. Patented for both its shape and functionality, the shoe anticipated an evolution in the sector, which later became common in snowboarding.

JASMINA KALUDEROVIC x ROSSIGNOL

Sketches for the restyling of the Rossignol Course ski boot

1994

Mixed media rendering:
Pantone and colored pencils on grey pape
Courtesy Jasmina Kaluderovic

Study for the aesthetic and functional modernization of the Rossignol Course racing boot, a model used in the 1980s by Slovenian skier Bojan Križaj, Alberto Tomba's rival at the time. Athletes wore boots designed with television coverage in mind: The color of the competition models was chosen to ensure maximum visibility and identification during races. The restyling followed trends in form and color inspired by car design, based on research that identified the boot as an extension of the skier's ideal car.

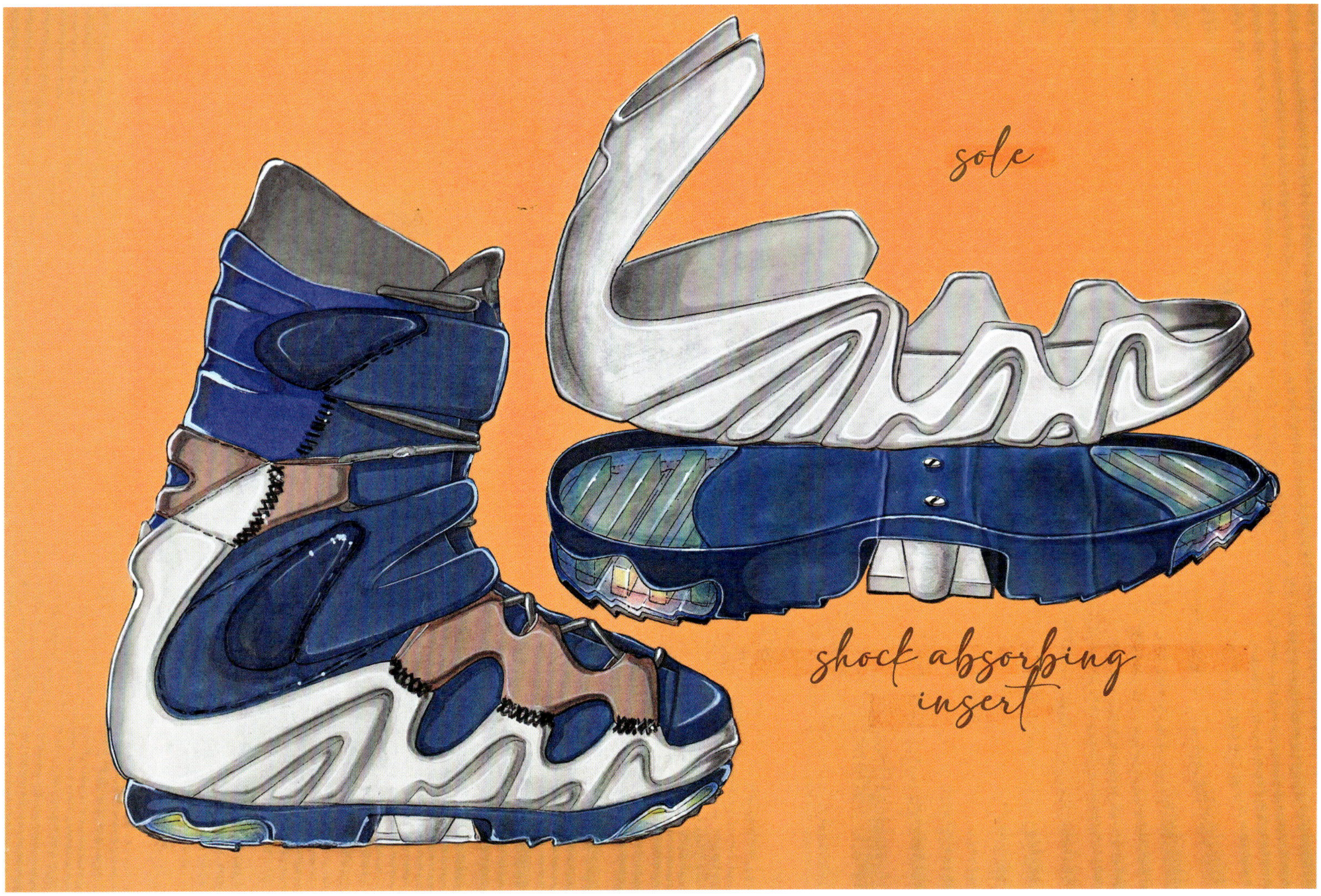

sole

shock absorbing insert

ROSSELLA GOLDSCHMIED x GOLDIE
Snow suit
c. 1990

Massa Lombarda, Archivi Mazzini

CHÖRBSCHHORN [CH]

SWATCH
Ski Patrol
1998

Courtesy Swatch

In 1998, Swatch presented the Ski Patrol model, part of the Access Snowpass collection—watches equipped with an integrated chip for access to various ski areas.

ATOMIC
Hans Kammerlander
1996

Color print
Courtesy Atomic

On May 24, 1996, Hans Kammerlander achieved a feat that had never been attempted before: He reached the summit of Everest alone, in 16 hours and 40 minutes, without oxygen. He then descended the north face to the advanced base camp on a pair of Atomic skis. He had already made the first descent on skis from Nanga Parbat in 1990. But it was on Everest that Kammerlander finally combined his three passions—climbing, mountaineering, and skiing—in a single line, making a descent that went down in mountaineering history.

PRADA
Men's coat and Suit
Fall/Winter 2007

Massa Lombarda, Archivi Mazzini

PYEONGCHANG [KR]

DELINEODESIGN
Torch for the Alpiniadi
2014

Wood and steel
Courtesy Delineodesign

Founded in 1999 by Giampaolo Allocco, Delineodesign is an industrial design studio based in Montebelluna, in the heart of the global manufacturing district linked to sports and the outdoors. The studio stands out for its cross-disciplinary approach to design, combining product design, visual communication, and identity development. At the heart of every project is the relationship between function, technology, language, and strategic skills: a creative synthesis that focuses on the essential, the effective, and the innovative. With over twenty-five years of experience and collaborations with international brands, Delineodesign has transformed complex ideas into successful products, winning numerous awards including the Red Dot Design Award, the Good Design Award, the Pro Winter Award, the German Design Award, and two mentions at the Compasso d'Oro, one of which was part of the Compasso d'Oro International.

DELINEODESIGN
Sketches for the Torch for the Alpiniadi
2014

Pencil on paper
Courtesy Delineodesign

Designed in collaboration with Massimo Rosati for the event promoted by the Associazione Nazionale Alpini, the torch consists of two main elements: a solid natural oak handle and a brushed steel flame guard, laser cut and calendered. The flame guard echoes the stylized shape of the Alpine pen, with diagonal cuts that help to provide oxygen for the flame.

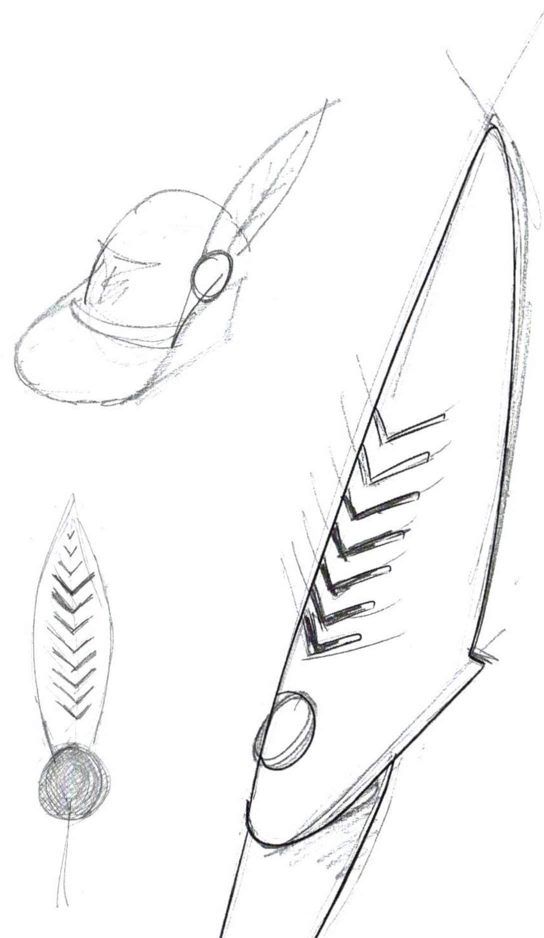

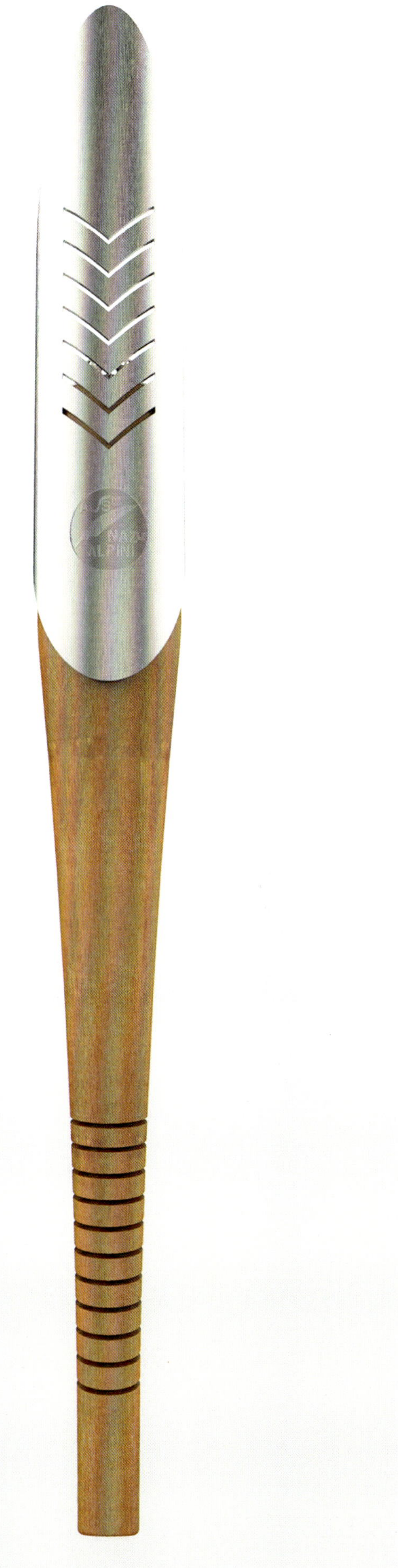

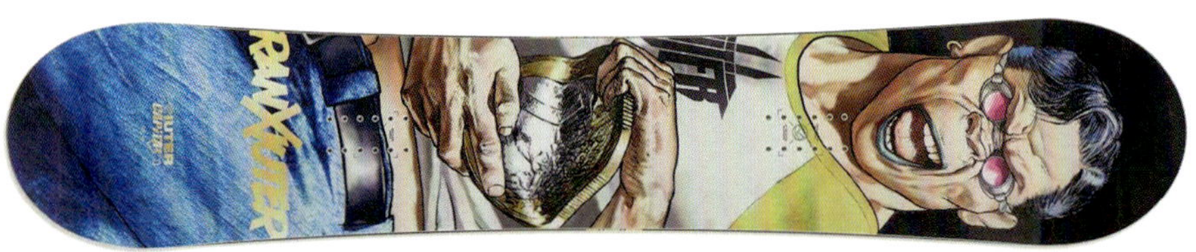

IUTER
Ranxiuter, snowboard, and snowboard bindings
2022

Courtesy IUTER

Part of the Euroiuter collection, the snowboard and the bindings are inspired by the visual imagery of Ranxerox, the famous cyberpunk character created in the late 1970s by Stefano Tamburini and Tanino Liberatore. The artwork features the iconic comic book character who appeared in the underground magazines *Cannibale* and *Frigidaire*, set in the slums of an apocalyptic Rome defined by urban decay and violence.

NOAH SALASNEK x SIMS
Noah's Ark snowboard
1995

Private Collection

STONE ISLAND
Padded jacket
Fall/Winter 2016

Massa Lombarda, Archivi Mazzini

MATTERHORN [IT] 

ENRIQUE LARIOS x BURTON
Hometown Hero Camber snowboard
2024

Private Collection

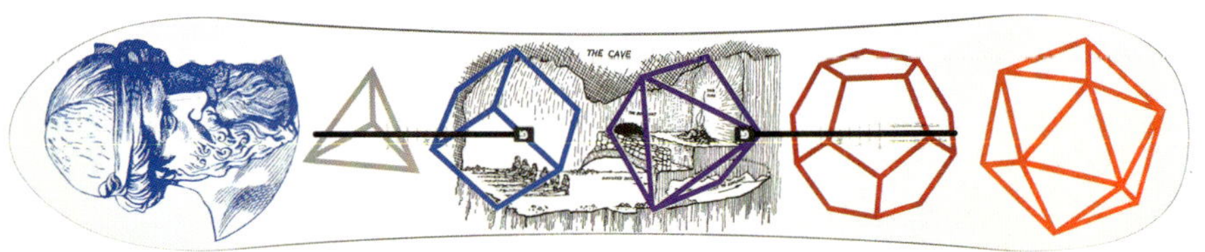

JEFF KOONS x BURTON
Philosopher snowboard
2016

Private Collection

SWATCH
Petits Batons
2018

SWATCH
Star Games
2018

SWATCH
Chinese Winter Scenery
2022

Courtesy Swatch

Since 1996, the centenary of the Olympic Games, which took place in Atlanta that year, Swatch has been the official timekeeper of the Olympics, renewing its partnership (Sydney 2000 and Athens 2004). Since then, it has continued to create watches for each game in collaboration with OMEGA and the IOC. For the 2018 Winter Games in PyeongChang, the brand launched the Star Games and Petits Batons models, inspired by the Korean logo made with Hangul letters.

TESSIER
Tempo Dualski
2014

Courtesy Tessier

In 1988, in Saint-Sorlin-d'Arves, Pierre Tessier developed the first sitski model, giving shape to a vision born from his encounter with the Association des Paralysés de France (now the APF France Handicap). His passion for skiing and mechanics led to the creation of the Tandemski, which went into production in 1995 with the founding of the Tessier company. This was followed by fundamental innovations for accessibility on snow: with various models of Uniski and Dualski, both for beginners and for the most competitive levels, such as Snow'Kart (special sitski), Eskaip (cross-country sled), Swaik (sitwake), Cimgo, and Trialp (all-terrain buggy).

TESSIER
Bastien Perret on the Tempo Dualski
2014

Courtesy Tessier

SALVATORE FERRAGAMO
Oslo
Pre/Fall 2017

Silk twill
Florence, Museo Ferragamo

SALVATORE FERRAGAMO
Oslo
Pre/Fall 2017

Silk twill
Florence, Museo Ferragamo

LOUIS VUITTON
Snowboard Vivienne
Keyring/Bag charm
2019

Private Collection

THOM BROWNE
Ankle boots
Fall/Winter 2016

Private Collection

DSQUARED2
Skate Moss *boots*
Fall/Winter 2011

Private Collection

CHANEL
Snow Gondola clutch bag
Fall/Winter 2019

Private Collection

PUCCI x FUSALP
Ski suit
2023

Courtesy Fusalp

JAAM x AMSI
Uniform for ski instructors
2021-2025

DESCENTE x AMSI
Uniform for ski instructors
2014-2018

BAILO x AMSI
Uniform for ski instructors
2010-2014

VUARNET x AMSI
Uniform for ski instructors
2007-2010

Courtesy AMSI

Founded on November 18, 1963 by Giampaolo Frigerio, Piero Bosticco, Vittorio Carpineti, Alberto Demetz, Renato Valle, and Guerrino Frigerio, AMSI (the Italian ski instructors association) was created with the aim of representing and upholding the role of ski instructors. Today, AMSI coordinates over 12,000 instructors and more than 400 schools throughout Italy.

BOGNER
Padded jacket with Vintage Archive print
c. 2010

Massa Lombarda, Archivi Mazzini

Founded in Munich in 1932 by Willy Bogner senior, the company began as an importer of skis and sports knitwear. In the 1940s, Maria Bogner shifted the company's focus towards fashion, introducing the famous stretch trousers with stirrups and known as Bogners in 1948 and the zip with the B logo, the brand's first distinctive logo, in 1955. In the 1960s and 1970s, Willy Bogner Jr. combined his work at the company with a career in cinema, as a consultant for the skiing scenes in several James Bond films.

KRASNAYA POLYANA [RU] 

SWATCH
Winner Ride
2009

Courtesy Swatch

In 2009, Swatch presented the CreArt collection with four models designed by Ted Scapa: Threesixty Ride, Winner Ride, Big Ride, and Pink Ride. The graphics, populated by small colorful snowboarders, reflect Scapa's typical visual language: stylized figures, essential lines, and a playful vitality that characterize all of his work. Born in Amsterdam in 1931 and active in Switzerland, Scapa was known for his work in art, publishing, and television, with a narrative style that was essential and immediate.

SWATCH
T'schuss
2016

Courtesy Swatch

SWATCH
Boarderage
2004

Courtesy Swatch

MARIANA FRANZETTI
The ABC's of Snowboarding
2024

Courtesy Mariana Franzetti

Created by illustrator and graphic designer Mariana Franzetti in collaboration with children's author and snowboarding enthusiast Neev Zaiet, *The ABCs of Snowboarding* is an illustrated book that combines learning the alphabet with an introduction to the world of snowboarding. Each letter of the alphabet is associated with a freestyle technique or movement.

STONE ISLAND—SERIES 100
Padded jacket
Fall/Winter 2000

Massa Lombarda, Archivi Mazzini

AQUILANO.RIMONDI
Padded biker jacket
Fall/Winter 2016

Massa Lombarda, Archivi Mazzini

ADIDAS
Y-3 Gendo Superstar
Spring/Summer 2023

Private Collection

JUNYA WATANABE
Padded coat
Fall/Winter 2023

Massa Lombarda, Archivi Mazzini

HIDA MOUNTAINS [JP] 

ATOMIC
Redster TR F5
2024

Courtesy Atomic

Lucas Pinheiro Braathen tests the Redster TR F5.

FUSALP
Uniforms for GB Snowsport
2021

Courtesy Fusalp

Since 2021, Fusalp is the official supplier of the British GB Snowsport team for alpine and para-alpine disciplines, including the 2022 Beijing Olympic Games and the 2023 World Championships in Courchevel-Méribel. In collaboration with the French technical studio Jonathan & Fletcher, Fusalp created racing suits and off-piste clothing.

ATOMIC
Redster TR F5
2024

Study sketches
Courtesy Atomic

Founded in 1955 by Alois Rohrmoser in Altenmarkt in the heart of the Austrian Alps, Atomic began as a small workshop, their first forty pairs of skis hand-carved from local wood. In just two years, production exceeded two thousand units, initiating a growth that would lead the brand to become a world leader in ski equipment. Among its innovations, in 1988 engineer Rupert Huber created the first powder skis inspired by snowboard design, the Powder Magic, which ushered in a new era of wide skis. Acquired by Amer Sports in 1994, Atomic continues to produce most of its models in Altenmarkt. Its successes on the ski slopes are associated with champions such as Hermann Maier, Mikaela Shiffrin, and Lucas Pinheiro Braathen.

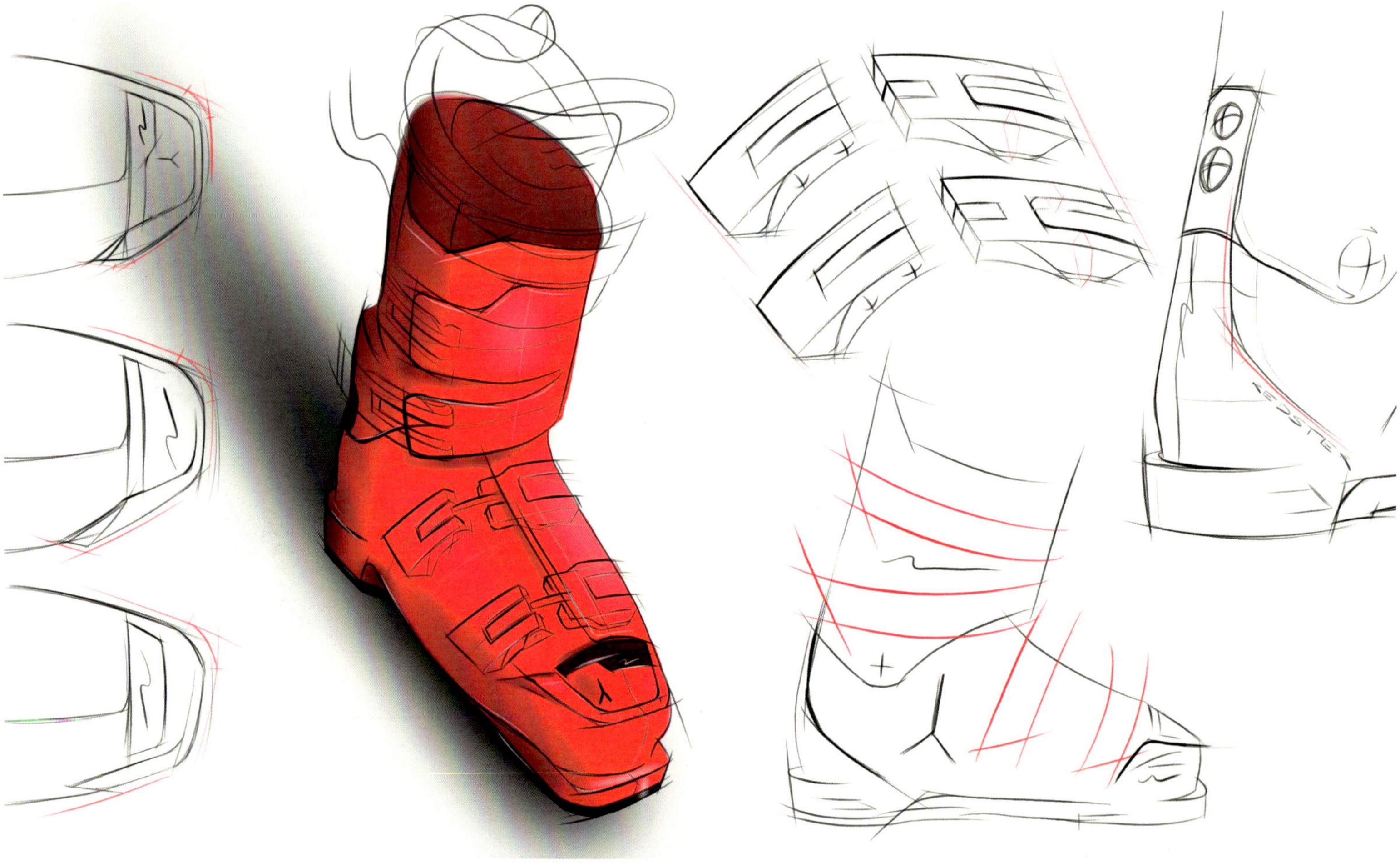

LEKI
Quinn Estates
GURGL
HESTRA

SARTORIA VICO
Wool suit: balaclava, jumper, and trousers
Wool suit: turtleneck, sweater, collar, trousers
Fall/Winter 2025

Courtesy Sartoria Vico

A Milanese brand founded by Cristina Del Buono and Stefania Casacci in 2011, Sartoria Vico offers essential and contemporary knitwear for women. The garments, made entirely in Italy with fine, sustainable yarns, combine formal minimalism and project research. The design of the garments stands out for its clean cuts, harmonious volumes, and vibrant palette of colors.

MASSIF DES ÉCRINS [FR]

extreme cashmere
St. Moritz Collection
2023

Courtesy extreme cashmere

Launched in 2016 by Saskia Dijkstra, extreme cashmere reinterprets knitwear with an essential language: unisex, one-size-fits-all garments that are not seasonal. The 2023 collection, designed for the snow, first appeared in St. Moritz with monochromatic outfits—from white to green, including pink and brown—characterized by soft volumes and minimal silhouettes.

RICK OWENS
Lunar Tractor Boots
2020

Private Collection

PLAN C
Men's outfit: sweater, trousers, and padded mittens
Women's outfit: cape and padded mittens, sweater and skirt
Fall/Winter 2025

Courtesy Plan C

Founded in Milan by Carolina Castiglioni in 2018, Plan C was born from the experience gained within the family business (Marni) and stands out for its formal research combining masculine and feminine elements, experimentation with materials and color. A love of mountains, particularly the Engadine, a place that is part of the designer's own personal experience, emerges in various aspects of the creative project: in the sporty details that run through the collections and in the photographic prints of the Spring/Summer 2021 collection, inspired by the landscapes of Celerina, reinterpreted as graphic collages that capture the spirit and colors of alpine nature.

PIZ NAIR [CH] 

JUNYA WATANABE
Padded jacket
Fall/Winter 2023

Massa Lombarda, Archivi Mazzini

PLAN C
Padded shoes
Fall/Winter 2025

Courtesy Plan C

MONCLER + RICK OWENS
Radiance Peter Jacket
2024

Private Collection

DELINEODESIGN x K2
Mindbender BOA
2024

Courtesy Delineodesign

Founded in 1962 in Washington State by Bill and Don Kirschner, K2 was the first American company to successfully introduce fiberglass into ski manufacturing. Originally a manufacturer of medical components, the company takes its name from the second highest peak in the world, as well as the initials of the two founding brothers. In 1964, K2 launched its first models and in 1969 became part of the history of alpine skiing with Marilyn Cochran's victory in the World Cup: it was the first title won on American skis. In the 1980s, the company expanded its range to include snowboarding and also became a pioneer in the design of specific equipment for women with the creation of the Women's Alliance™ in 1999. The collaboration between the American company and the Italian design studio led, among other things, to the creation of the Mindbender BOA model. This freeride boot is designed to tackle any terrain without compromising on control, comfort, or safety. The BOA® Fit system allows for precise micro-adjustment of the fit, adapting to the shape of the foot to maximize sensitivity and reduce pressure points. The FastFit insert on the instep makes it easy to get in and out, while the Y-shaped rear support and Powerlock Spyne mechanism ensure lateral stiffness, downhill efficiency, and responsiveness on fresh snow. Thanks to its technical innovation and functional design, Mindbender BOA received a mention at the Compasso d'Oro ADI 2024 and the Prowinter Award Retail 2024.

DELINEODESIGN x K2
Mindbender BOA
2024

Study sketches
Courtesy Delineodesign

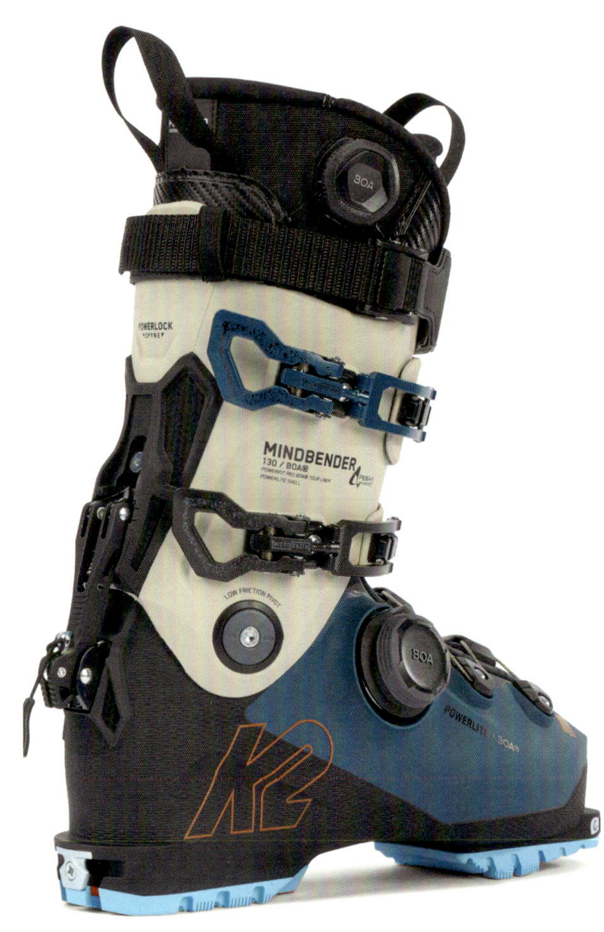

POWERLITE x BOA
K2

MILANO
Cortina

RICCARDO GUASCO x ESSELUNGA
Slalom
2025

Courtesy Riccardo Guasco

An illustrator born in Alessandria, Riccardo Guasco combines poetry and irony in an essential style inspired by Cubism, Futurism, and Russian Suprematism. His works, identifiable in their use of simple shapes and powerful colors, appear on posters, magazines, books, ships, and bicycles. He has collaborated with *The New Yorker*, Esselunga, Rai, Ferrari, Emergency, Greenpeace, Longines, Poste Italiane, Rapha, and Moby, and has received international awards such as the ILLUSTRI Prize 2019 and two Silver Medals at the AI Annual Awards.

RICCARDO GUASCO x ESSELUNGA
Dynamism of a Double Bobsleigh
2025

Courtesy Riccardo Guasco

RICCARDO GUASCO x SIX SENSES KITZBUHEL RESIDENCES
Untitled
2025

Courtesy Riccardo Guasco

[FR] CHAMONIX | 1924
260 ATHLETES

[CH] ST. MORITZ | 1928
464 ATHLETES

[US] LAKE PLACID | 1932
252 ATHLETES

[DE] GARMISCH-PARTENKIRCHEN | 1936
646 ATHLETES

[CH] ST. MORITZ | 1948
669 ATHLETES

[NO] OSLO | 1952
694 ATHLETES

[IT] CORTINA D'AMPEZZO | 1956
821 ATHLETES

[US] SQUAW VALLEY | 1960
665 ATHLETES

[AU] INNSBRUCK | 1964
1091 ATHLETES

[FR] GRENOBLE | 1968
1158 ATHLETES

[JP] SAPPORO | 1972
1006 ATHLETES

[AU] INNSBRUCK | 1976
1123 ATHLETES

[SE] ÖRNSKÖLDSVIK | 1976
196 ATHLETES

[US] LAKE PLACID | 1980
1072 ATHLETES

[NO] GEILO | 1980
299 ATHLETES

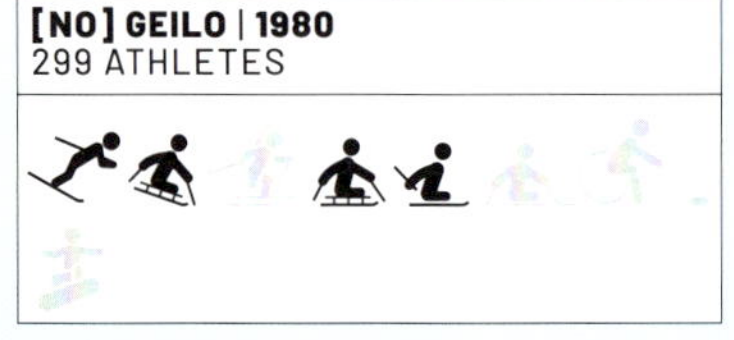

[YU] SARAJEVO | 1984
1272 ATHLETES

[AU] INNSBRUCK | 1984
419 ATHLETES

[CA] CALGARY | 1984
1423 ATHLETES

[AU] INNSBRUCK | 1988
377 ATHLETES

[FR] ALBERTVILLE | 1992
1801 ATHLETES

[FR] ALBERTVILLE AND TIGNES | 1992
365 ATHLETES

[NO] LILLEHAMMER | 1994
1737 ATHLETES

[NO] LILLEHAMMER | 1994
471 ATHLETES

[JP] NAGANO | 1998
2176 ATHLETES

[JP] NAGANO | 1998
571 ATHLETES

[US] SALT LAKE CITY | 2002
2399 ATHLETES

[US] SALT LAKE CITY | 2002
416 ATHLETES

[IT] TURIN | 2006
2508 ATHLETES

[IT] TURIN | 2006
486 ATHLETES

[CA] VANCOUVER | 2010
2566 ATHLETES

[CA] VANCOUVER | 2010
506 ATHLETES

[RU] SOCHI | 2014
2780 ATHLETES

[RU] SOCHI | 2014
550 ATHLETES

[KR] PYEONGCHANG | 2018
2833 ATHLETES

[KR] PYEONGCHANG | 2018
569 ATHLETES

[CN] BEIJING | 2022
2834 ATHLETES

[CN] BEIJING | 2022
564 ATHLETES

[IT] MILANO-CORTINA | 2026
____ ATHLETES

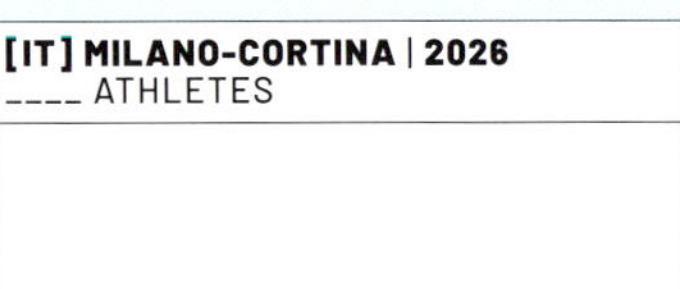

[FR] FRENCH ALPS | 2026
____ ATHLETES

[US] SALT LAKE CITY-UTAH | 2030
____ ATHLETES

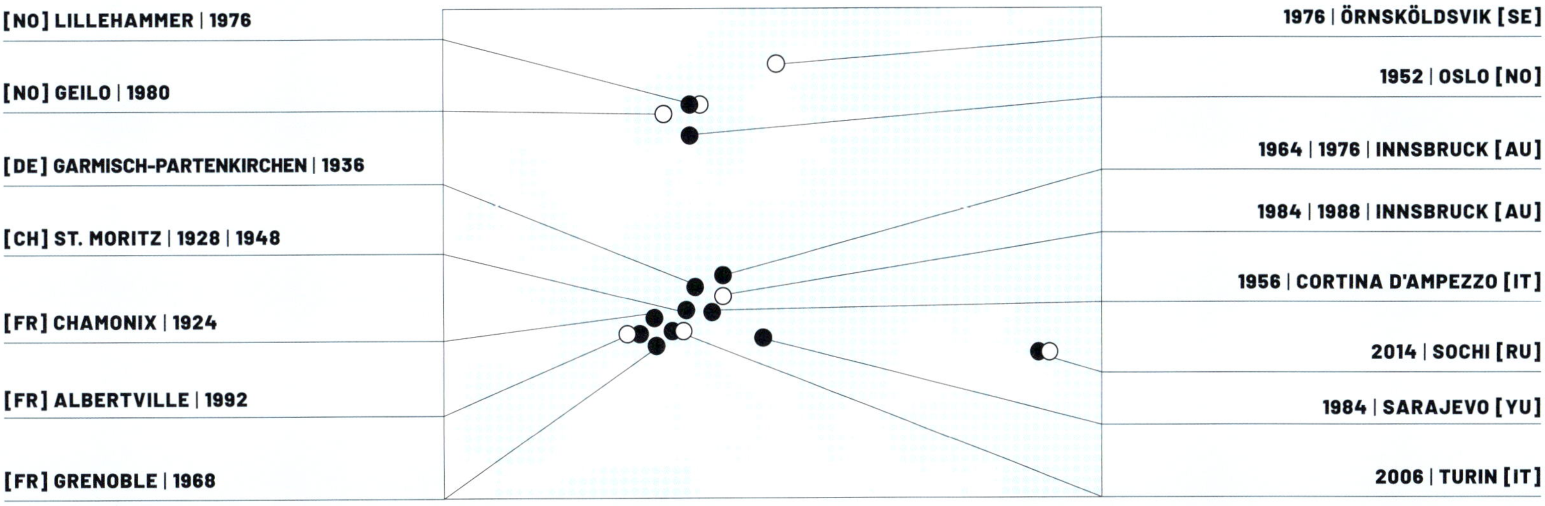

[NO] LILLEHAMMER | 1976
[NO] GEILO | 1980
[DE] GARMISCH-PARTENKIRCHEN | 1936
[CH] ST. MORITZ | 1928 | 1948
[FR] CHAMONIX | 1924
[FR] ALBERTVILLE | 1992
[FR] GRENOBLE | 1968

1976 | ÖRNSKÖLDSVIK [SE]
1952 | OSLO [NO]
1964 | 1976 | INNSBRUCK [AU]
1984 | 1988 | INNSBRUCK [AU]
1956 | CORTINA D'AMPEZZO [IT]
2014 | SOCHI [RU]
1984 | SARAJEVO [YU]
2006 | TURIN [IT]

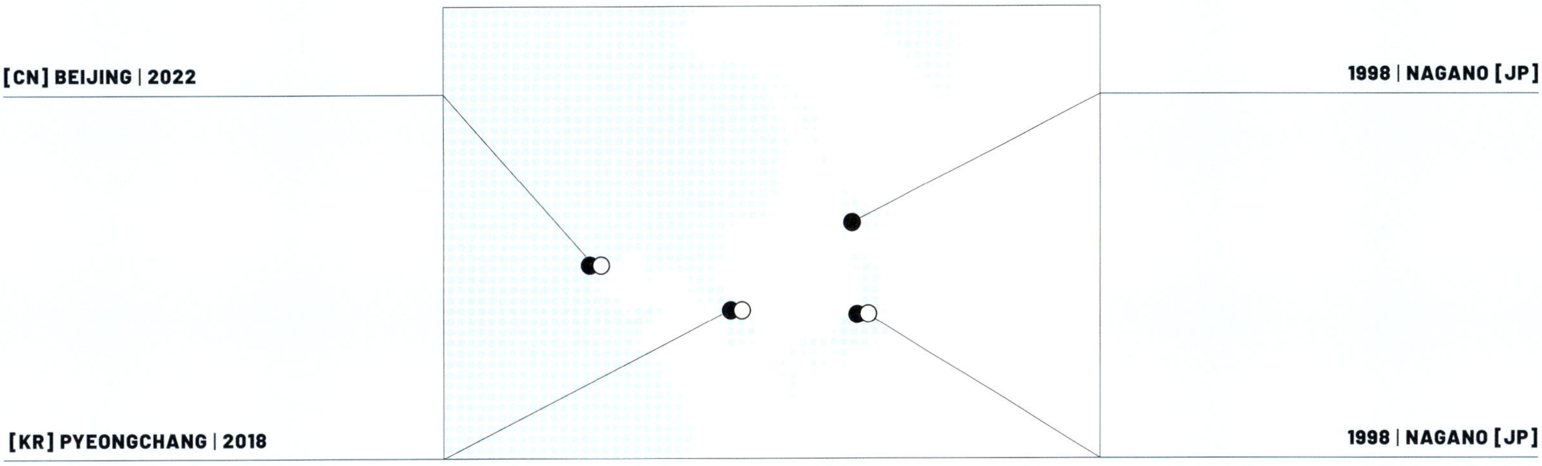

[CN] BEIJING | 2022
[KR] PYEONGCHANG | 2018

1998 | NAGANO [JP]
1998 | NAGANO [JP]

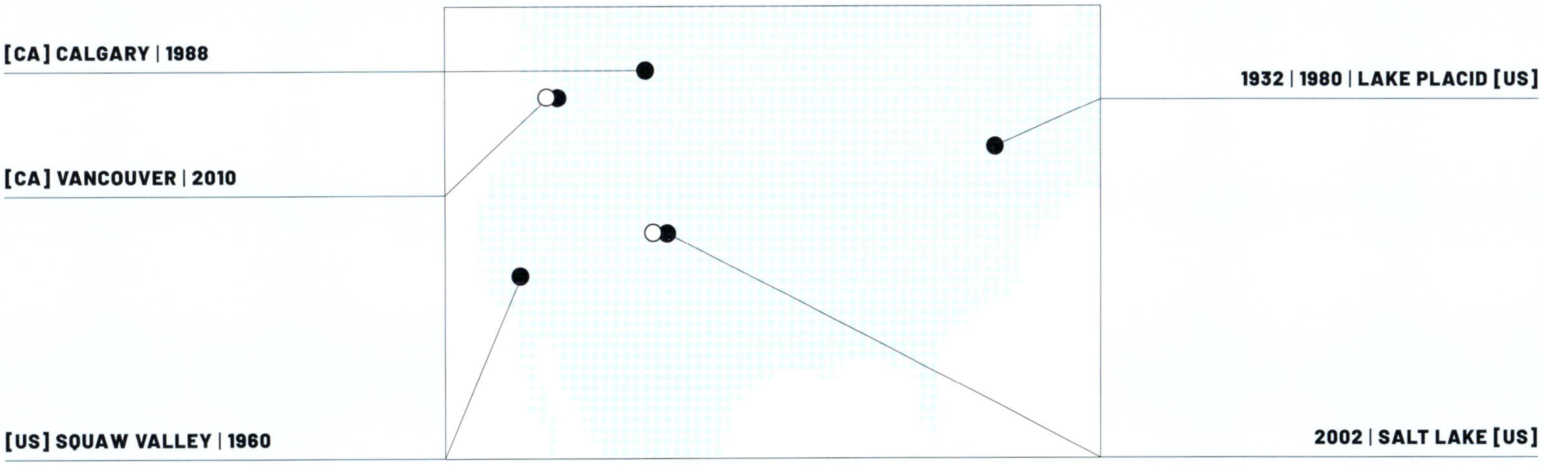

[CA] CALGARY | 1988
[CA] VANCOUVER | 2010
[US] SQUAW VALLEY | 1960

1932 | 1980 | LAKE PLACID [US]
2002 | SALT LAKE [US]

LEGEND

Figure Skating
Speed Skating
Ice Hockey
Short Track
Curling
Alpine Skiing
Ski Jumping
Nordic Combined
Luge / Skeleton
Bobsleigh
Cross Country Skiing
Freestyle Skiing
Snowboard Para Snowboard
Para Alpine Skiing
Sledge Downhill Racing
Biathlon Para Biathlon
Ice Sledge Speed Racing
Para Cross Country Skiing
Para Ice Hockey
Wheelchair Curling

Winter Olympic Games and Paralympic Games
Winter Olympic Games
Winter Paralympic Games

The data relating to the Olympic Games and Paralympic Winter Games were obtained from www.olympics.com, www.paralympic.org, and bibliographic sources concerning various editions of the Winter Olympics. The numbers of medals listed on the following pages are the mathematical sum of all those won in the various disciplines by each country.

1924
CHAMONIX [FR]
0/25/01 - 05/02/1924

TEAMS **16**
DISCIPLINES **9**
EVENTS **16**

0/MEDAL TABLE
01 NORWAY
02 FINLAND
03 USA / UK

Auguste Matisse

Raoul Bénard

1928
ST. MORITZ [CH]
0/11/02 - 19/02/1928

TEAMS **25**
DISCIPLINES **8**
EVENTS **14**

0/MEDAL TABLE
01 NORWAY
02 USA
03 SWEDEN

Hugo Laubi

Arnold Hunerwadel

1932
LAKE PLACID [US]
0/04/02 - 13/02/1932

TEAMS **17**
DISCIPLINES **7**
EVENTS **14**

0/MEDAL TABLE
01 USA
02 NORWAY
03 CANADA

Witold Gordon

Unknown designer

1936
GARMISCH-PARTENKIRCHEN [DE]
0/06/02 - 16/02/1936

TEAMS **28**
DISCIPLINES **8**
EVENTS **17**

0/MEDAL TABLE
01 NORWAY
02 SWEDEN
03 GERMANY/FINLAND

Ludwig Hohlwein

Richard Klein

1948
ST. MORITZ [CH]
0/30/01 - 08/02/1948

TEAMS **28**
DISCIPLINES **9**
EVENTS **22**

0/MEDAL TABLE
01 NORWAY/SWEDEN SWITZERLAND
02 USA
03 AUSTRIA

Fritz Hellinger

Paul-André Droz

1952
OSLO [NO]
0/14/02 - 25/02/1952

TEAMS **30**
DISCIPLINES **8**
EVENTS **22**

0/MEDAL TABLE
01 NORWAY
02 USA
03 FINLAND

Knut Yran

Vasos Falireus / Knut Yran

Geir Grung

1956
CORTINA D'AMPEZZO [IT]
0/26/01 - 05/02/1956

TEAMS **32**
DISCIPLINES **8**
EVENTS **24**

0/MEDAL TABLE
01 USSR
02 AUSTRIA
03 SWEDEN

Franco Rondinelli

Costantino Affer

Ralph Lavers

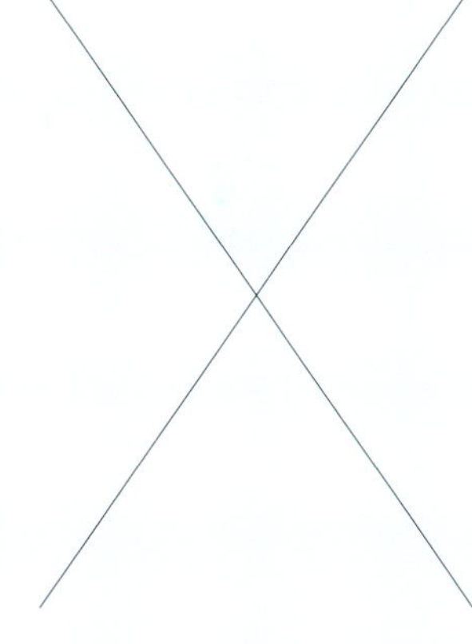

1960
SQUAW VALLEY [US]
0/18/02 - 28/02/1960

TEAMS **30**
DISCIPLINES **8**
EVENTS **27**

0/MEDAL TABLE
01 USSR
02 USA
03 GERMANY/FINLAND

James Charles Knollin

Unknown designer

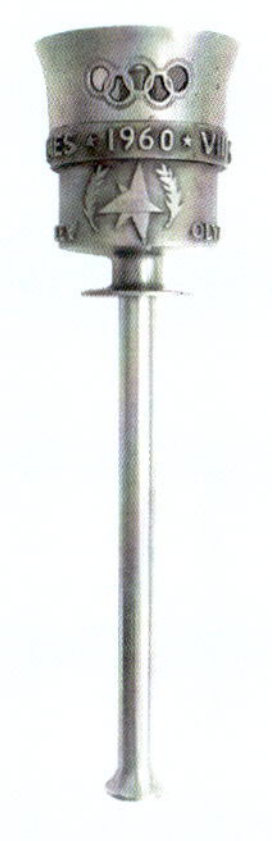

John Hench - Ralph Lavers

1964
INNSBRUCK [AU]
O/29/01 - 09/02/1964

TEAMS **36**
DISCIPLINES **10**
EVENTS **34**

O/MEDAL TABLE
01 USSR
02 NORWAY
03 AUSTRIA

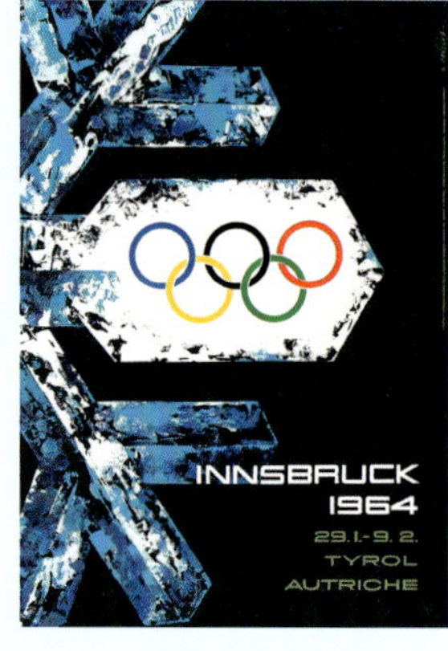

Wilhelm Jaruska

Martha Coufal-Hartl - Arthur Zelger

Ludwig Haselwanter

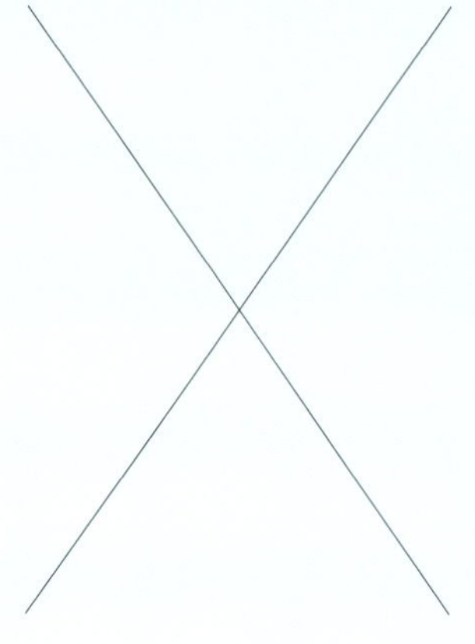

1968
GRENOBLE [FR]
O/06/02 - 18/02/1968

TEAMS **37**
DISCIPLINES **10**
EVENTS **35**

O/MEDAL TABLE
01 NORWAY
02 USSR
03 AUSTRIA

Roger Excoffon

Roger Excoffon

Unknown designer

Shuss /Aline Lafargue

1972
SAPPORO [JP]
O/03/02 - 13/02/1972

TEAMS **35**
DISCIPLINES **10**
EVENTS **35**

O/MEDAL TABLE
01 USSR
02 GDR
03 NORWAY

Takashi Kono

Yagi Kazumi - Ikko Tanaka

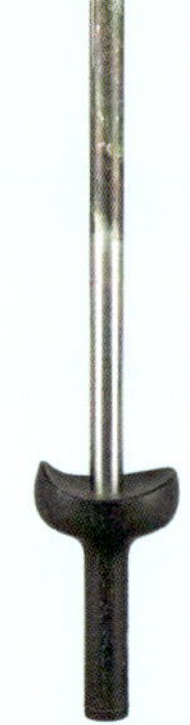
Munemichi Yanagi

unofficial
Takuchan / SEIKO design dept.

1976
INNSBRUCK [AU]
O/04/02 - 15/02/1976
P*/21/02 - 28/02/1976

TEAMS **37/16**
DISCIPLINES **10/2**
EVENTS **37/53**

O/MEDAL TABLE
01 USSR
02 GDR
03 USA/BRD

P/MEDAL TABLE
01 AUSTRIA
02 FRG
03 FINLAND

* ÖRNSKÖLDSVIK [SE]

Arthur Zelger

Martha Coufal-Hartl - Arthur Zelger

Unknown designer

Schneemandl / Walter Pötsch

1980
LAKE PLACID [US]
O/13/02 - 24/02/1980
P*/1/02 - 7/02/1980

TEAMS	**37/18**
DISCIPLINES	**10/2**
EVENTS	**38/63**

O/MEDAL TABLE
01 GDR
02 USSR
03 USA

P/MEDAL TABLE
01 AUSTRIA
02 NORWAY
03 SWITZERLAND

* GEILO [NO]

Robert W. Whitney

Tiffany & Co.

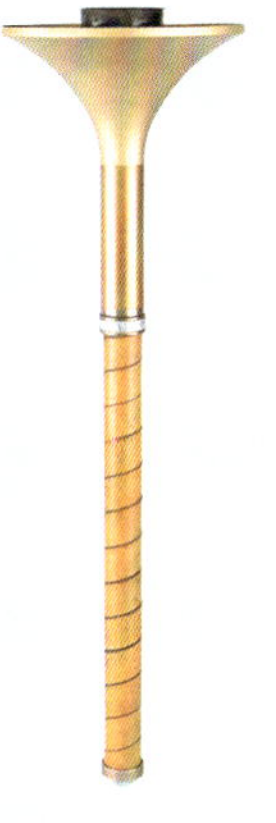
Don McFarland - McFarland Design

Roni / Don Moss - Capital Sports

1984
SARAJEVO [YU]
O/08/02 - 19/02/1984
P*/14/01 - 20/01/1984

TEAMS	**49/21**
DISCIPLINES	**10/3**
EVENTS	**39/107**

O/MEDAL TABLE
01 USSR
02 GDR
03 FINLAND

P/MEDAL TABLE
01 AUSTRIA
02 NORWAY
03 SWITZERLAND

* INNSBRUCK [AT]

Radmila Jovandić - Lora Levi

Nebojša Mitrić

Unknown designer

Vučko / Jože Trobec

1988
CALGARY [CA]
O/13/02 - 28/02/1988
P*/17/01 - 24/01/1988

TEAMS	**57/22**
DISCIPLINES	**10/4**
EVENTS	**46/96**

O/MEDAL TABLE
01 USSR
02 GDR
03 SWITZERLAND

P/MEDAL TABLE
01 NORWAY
02 AUSTRIA
03 BRD/USA

* INNSBRUCK [AT]

Justason & Tavender

Friedrich Peter

National Research Council of Canada

Hidy e Howdy / Sheila Scott

1992
ALBERTVILLE [FR]
O/08/02 - 23/02/1992
P/25/03 - 02/04/1992

TEAMS	**64/24**
DISCIPLINES	**12/3**
EVENTS	**57/79**

O/MEDAL TABLE
01 GERMANY
02 UNIFIED TEAM
03 AUSTRIA

P/MEDAL TABLE
01 USA
02 GERMANY
03 UNIFIED TEAM

Alain Doré - Florence Meschino

Marie-Claude Lalique Dedouvre

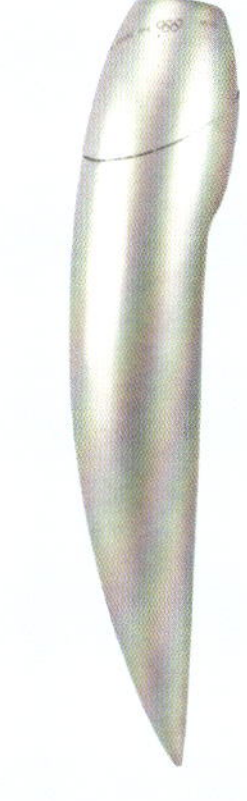
Philippe Starck

Magique / Philippe Mairesse

1994
LILLEHAMMER [NO]
O/12/02 - 27/02/1994
P/10/03 - 19/03/1994

TEAMS **67/31**
DISCIPLINES **12/5**
EVENTS **61/34**

O/MEDAL TABLE
01 NORWAY
02 GERMANY
03 RUSSIA

P/MEDAL TABLE
01 NORWAY
02 GERMANY/USA
03 AUSTRIA

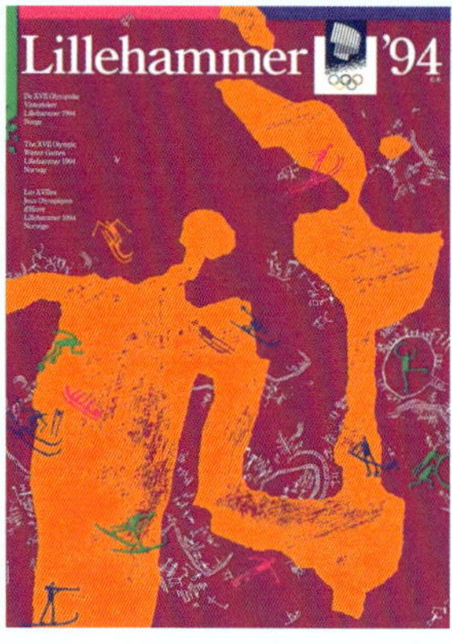

Ashley Booth - Sarah E. Rosenbaum

Ingjerd Hanevold

André Steenbuch Marandon
Paal Christian Kahrs

Håkon and Kristin
Kari and Werner Grossman
Original concept by J. R. Campuzano

1998
NAGANO [JP]
O/07/02 - 22/02/1998
P/07/03 - 16/03/1998

TEAMS **72/32**
DISCIPLINES **14/5**
EVENTS **68/34**

O/MEDAL TABLE
01 GERMANY
02 NORWAY
03 RUSSIA

P/MEDAL TABLE
01 GERMANY
02 JAPAN
03 NORWAY

Masuteru Aoba

Takeshi Ito

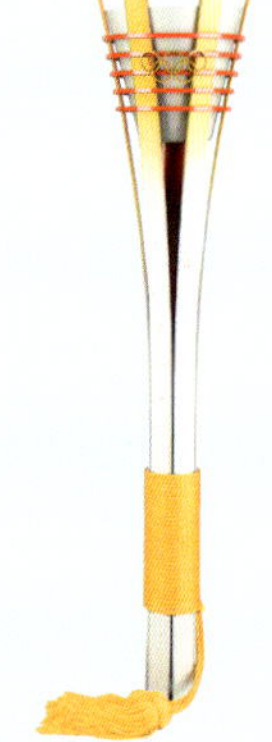
Nagano Olympic Games
Organising Committee

Sukki, Nokki, Lekki and Tsukki
Landor Associates

2002
SALT LAKE [US]
O/08/02 - 24/02/2002
P/09/03 - 18/03/2002

TEAMS **77/36**
DISCIPLINES **15/5**
EVENTS **78/58**

O/MEDAL TABLE
01 GERMANY
02 USA
03 NORWAY

P/MEDAL TABLE
01 USA
02 GERMANY
03 AUSTRIA

Justin Reynolds - Axiom Design

Scott Given - Axiom Design

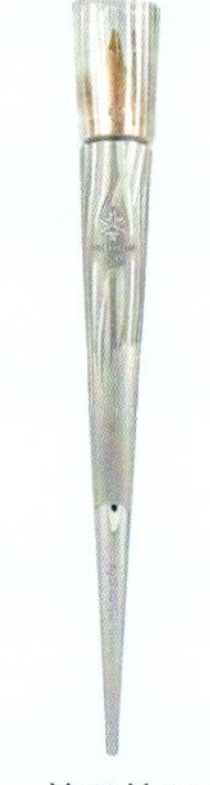
Scott Given - Matt Manes
Axiom Design

Powder, Coal and Copper
Landor/Publicis

2006
TORINO [IT]
O/10/02 - 26/02/2006
P/12/03 - 21/03/2006

TEAMS **80/39**
DISCIPLINES **15/5**
EVENTS **84/58**

O/MEDAL TABLE
01 GERMANY
02 USA
03 CANADA

P/MEDAL TABLE
01 RUSSIA
02 UKRAINE
03 GERMANY

Armando Testa

Dario Quatrini

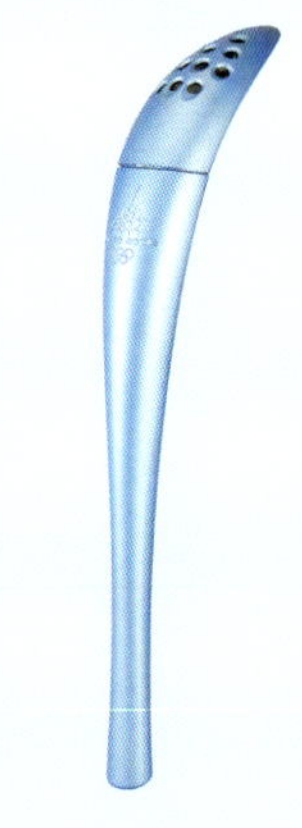
Pininfarina

Neve and Gliz / Pedro Albuquerque

2010
VANCOUVER [CA]
O/12/02 - 28/02/2010
P/12/03 - 21/03/2010

TEAMS **82/44**
DISCIPLINES **15/5**
EVENTS **86/64**

O/MEDAL TABLE
01 USA
02 GERMANY
03 CANADA

P/MEDAL TABLE
01 RUSSIA
02 GERMANY
03 UKRAINE/CANADA

Ben Hulse

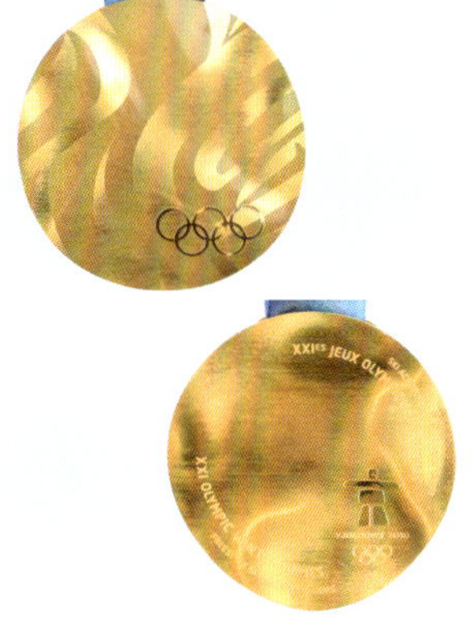
Omer Arbel - Corinne Hunt

Bombardier - VANOC

Quatchi e Miga / Meomi design

2014
SOCHI [RU]
O/07/02 - 23/02/2014
P/07/03 - 16/03/2014

TEAMS **88/45**
DISCIPLINES **15/5**
EVENTS **98/72**

O/MEDAL TABLE
01 RUSSIA
02 USA
03 NORWAY

P/MEDAL TABLE
01 RUSSIA
02 UKRAINE
03 USA

Unknown designer

Leo Burnett

Vladimir Pirozhkov - Andrei Vodyanik

La lepre, l'orso polare e il leopardo
S. Petrova - O. Seredechniy - V. Pak

2018
PYEONGCHANG [KR]
O/09/02 - 25/02/2018
P/09/03 - 18/03/2018

TEAMS **92/46**
DISCIPLINES **15/6**
EVENTS **102/80**

O/MEDAL TABLE
01 NORWAY
02 GERMANY
03 CANADA

P/MEDAL TABLE
01 USA
02 CANADA
03 NEUTRAL PARALYMPIC ATHLETES

Ha Jong-joo

Lee Suk-woo

Young Se Kim

Soohorang / So-Young Park

2022
BEIJING [CN]
O/04/02 - 20/02/2022
P/04/03 - 13/04/2022

TEAMS **91/46**
DISCIPLINES **15/6**
EVENTS **109/78**

O/MEDAL TABLE
01 NORWAY
02 ROC
03 GERMANY

P/MEDAL TABLE
01 CHINA
02 UKRAINE
03 CANADA

Lin Cunzhen

Unknown designer

Team creativo di Alibaba

Bing Dwen Dwen and Shuey Rhon Rhon
Cao Xue

PHOTO CREDITS

All photographs of the clothes in the Archivi Mazzini in Massa Lombarda are by Alessandro Dealberto Photography, Milan

© Apic/Getty Images: p. 48 right
© Archivio Fotografico Centro Studi Vetro/Archivio Guido Balsamo Stella, Venice: p. 69
© Archivio Fotografico Fondazione Musei Civici di Venezia: pp. 22, 59 left
© Archivio Freyrie, Milan: p. 70
© Archivio Italo Sport, Milan: pp. 134, 135, 143 right, 171 right, 176
© Archivio Missoni: endpapers, pp. 145 left, 164, 165, 192, 193, 194
© Archivio Prodotti Fondazione Sportsystem, Montebelluna: pp. 18, 30 left, 74 bottom, 104, 113, 136 bottom, 138 bottom, 156 top, 156 bottom, 170, 173, 183
© Arnaud de Rosnay/Conde Nast via Getty Images: p. 155 bottom
© Biblioteka Jagiellonska, Krakow: p. 67
© Bibliothèque National de France, Paris: pp. 44 top right, 45, 48 left, 82, 142 right, 143 left
© Bridgeman Images: pp. 51, 93
© Carl Iwasaki/Getty Images: p. 149
© Christie's Images, London/Bridgeman Images: p. 56
© Dalarnas museum, Falun: p. 181
© Digital image, The Museum of Modern Art, New York/Scala, Florence: pp. 186 bottom left, 186 bottom right
© Film Publicity Archive/United Archives via Getty Images: p. 153
© Fondazione Antonio Ratti, Como: pp. 11 left, 29, 122 top right, 122 bottom right, 123, 144 left
© Foto Archivio Rossignol: pp. 102, 103, 160 top, 160 bottom, 168 left, 168 right, 168 bottom, 186
© Foto Scala, Florence/bpk, Bildagentur für Kunst, Kultur und Geschichte, Berlin: p. 46
© Foto Scala, Florence/V&A Images/Victoria and Albert Museum, London: p. 52
© Helsingin kaupunginmuseo, Helsinki: p. 78
© Jean-Claude Sauer/Paris Match via Getty Images: p. 11 right
© KHM, Vienna: p. 58 right
© Kunstindustrimuseet, Oslo: pp. 35, 53
© Library of Congress, Washington: pp. 30 center, 122 top left, 122 bottom left, 157
© Musée McCord Stewart, Montreal: pp. 9 left, 25, 26, 27, 30 bottom, 31, 44 bottom right, 54, 142 center
© Musée National du Sport, Paris: pp. 33, 42 top, 44 top left, 44 bottom left, 72 bottom
© Museo Ferragamo, Florence: pp. 177, 212, 213
© Museum für Kunst und Gewerbe Hamburg, Hamburg: p. 80
© Museum of Fine Arts, Boston: p. 41
© Museum Rotterdam, Rotterdam: pp. 16, 39
© Muzeum Narodowe w Warszawie, Warsaw: p. 37
© Narodowe Archiwum Cyfrowe, Warsaw: p. 47 top
© Nasjonalmuseet, Oslo: p. 181
© National Galleries of Scotland/Bridgeman Images: p. 21
© National Gallery of Victoria, Melbourne: p. 96
© Nordiska museet, Stockholm: pp. 47 bottom left, 47 bottom right, 81 bottom, 92
© ONB, Vienna: p. 74 top
© Popperfoto via Getty Images: p. 150 bottom
© Powerhouse Museum, Sydney: p. 28 top
© Public Library, Boston: p. 106
© Public Library, New York: p. 109
© Raffaello Pernici, Rosignano Marittimo: pp. 42 bottom, 50 top left, 50 bottom left, 55, 72, 73, 87, 90, 97, 121 left
© Rijksmuseum, Amsterdam: p. 17
© RMN-Grand Palais/René-Gabriel Ojéda/Dist. Foto Scala, Florence: p. 58 center
© Shutterstock: pp. 31, 53, 71, 83, 101, 139, 154, 163, 169, 172, 180, 185, 187, 191, 195, 199, 200, 204, 206, 209, 217, 221, 224, 227
© Slim Aarons/Hulton Archive/Getty Images: p. 140
© Staten Museum for Kunst, Copenhagen: p. 19
© Szukaj w Archiwach, Warsaw: p. 81 top
© The Art Institute, Chicago: pp. 20 top, 20 bottom
© The Metropolitan Museum of Art, New York: pp. 24, 28 bottom
© The National Gallery, London/Scala, Florence: p. 59 right
© The National Museum of Modern Art, Kyoto: p. 61 left
© Turun kaupunginmuseo, Turku: p. 78
© UCLA, Los Angeles: pp. 121 top, 121 bottom, 159
© Varmlands Museum, Varmlands: p. 77
© Yasuiko Kobayashi/SKIER Magazine, Yama to Keikoku Sha: pp. 196, 197
Courtesy AMSI: p. 216
Courtesy Archivio Jacovitti: pp. 116-117
Courtesy Archivio Renata Fusi, Silvana Mollica, Paolo Zanotto Architetti Associati: pp. 188, 189 top, 189 bottom, 190, 201 top, 201 bottom
Courtesy Aste Boetto, Genoa: p. 68
Courtesy Atomic: pp. 7, 205 bottom, 222 top, 222 bottom
Courtesy Calze GM: pp. 162 top, 162 bottom
Courtesy Cambi Casa d'Aste, Milan: pp. 50 top right, 50 bottom right
Courtesy Delineodesign: pp. 207 top, 207 bottom, 228 top, 228 bottom, 229
Courtesy Dolomite: pp. 112, 138 top, 174
Courtesy extreme cashmere: p. 225
Courtesy Fusalp: pp. 147 left, 178, 179, 215, 223
Courtesy Il Ponte Casa d'Aste, Milan: pp. 64, 94, 99
Courtesy IUTER: pp. 15 left, 208 top
Courtesy Jasmina Kaluderovic: pp. 15 right, 202 top, 202 bottom, 203 top, 203 bottom
Courtesy Mariana Franzetti: p. 219
Courtesy Riccardo Guasco: pp. 15 center, 230, 231 top, 231 bottom
Courtesy Swatch: pp. 13 right, 184 top, 205 top, 210, 218
Courtesy Tecnica Group: pp. 151 left, 151 right, 166 left, 166 right, 182
Courtesy Tessier: pp. 211 top, 211 bottom

The Publisher and Authors thank all private collectors and archives who kindly made their photographic material available.

Every reasonable attempt has been made to identify owners of copyright. Errors or omissions notified to the publisher will be corrected in subsequent editions.

REPRODUCTION AND PRINTING

Grafiche Antiga S.p.A., Crocetta del Montello, TV
for Marsilio Arte srl, Venice

ermatt
Chamonix